The Adoptive Family as a Healing Resource for the Sexually Abused Child

MW01688773

The Adoptive Family as a Healing Resource for the Sexually Abused Child: A Training Manual

Deborah H. Minshew
and Chrisan Hooper

Child Welfare League of America
Washington, DC

Copyright © 1990 by the Child Welfare League of America, Inc.

All Rights Reserved. Neither this book nor any part may be reproduced or transmitted in any form or by any means, electronic or mechanical, including photocopying, microfilming, and recording, or by any information storage and retrieval system, without permission in writing from the publisher. For information on this or other CWLA publications, contact the CWLA Publications Department at the address below.

CHILD WELFARE LEAGUE OF AMERICA, INC.
440 First Street, NW, Suite 310, Washington, DC 20001-2085

CURRENT PRINTING (last digit)
10 9 8 7 6 5 4 3 2 1

Cover design by Kevin Erskine
Text design by Eve Malakoff-Klein

Printed in the United States of America

ISBN # 0–87868–360–7

Research reveals that not everyone who suffers a damaging childhood grows up to be a damaged human being...

JUDITH VIORST
NECESSARY LOSSES

Contents

Introduction

Sexual abuse is the ultimate violation of childhood. Not only are children violated physically and denied the right of ownership of their own bodies, but they quickly learn that adults, in most cases parents, cannot be trusted. It is generally acknowledged by psychiatrists, psychologists, and child development specialists that the trust relationship between children and parents is absolutely essential to the children's emotional development, for upon this first trust relationship depends their future ability to give and receive love, as well as their view of themselves as persons worthy of being loved. As Viorst says [1986: 621], "We cannot love unless we know what love is. We cannot love others as others unless we possess sufficient self-love, a love we learn from being loved."

We are justifiably horrified by the physical aspects of sexual abuse, the pain inflicted on bodies not yet ready for sexual intimacy. We are especially horrified by the descriptions of sadistic sexual abuse where the intentional infliction of pain is a part of the arousal process for the adult involved. When it is a parent or trusted family member who is responsible for this pain, this "unnatural act," we find it hard to believe. It is easier to accept that child molesters are perverted strangers who snatch children off the street, because our values dictate that parents love their children, and we cannot resolve the concepts of parental love and sexual abuse of the child by the parent. We are confronted by the statistics, however, which inform us that less than 5% of the cases of sexual abuse of children involve strangers. In 70% to 80% of the cases the abuser is a family member, with the remainder of the abusers falling into the category of trusted adult (friend of the family, neighbor, Sunday school teacher, scout leader, etc.).

This dichotomy becomes easier to understand when we remember that we cannot love unless we know what love is, and we cannot love others unless we love ourselves. Sexually abusing parents frequently profess their love for their child, but they do not know what love is or how to express love. Sexually abusing parents do not really love themselves; they are therefore incapable of loving their child in a protective, mature relationship.

Recognizing the importance to the child of parental love, caring, and protection, and the devastation that sexual abuse is, we are incredulous to learn that most children not only survive the physical and emotional torment they suffer, but many become well-functioning adults. This does not mean that the sexual abuse has been forgotten; on the contrary, those who deny and suppress the abuse are generally not among the true survivors. Nor does it mean that there are no emotional scars. Rather, their survival is testament to the adaptability and recuperative powers of children. Many adult survivors have reported that one of the most important factors in their development was the discovery of an adult—friend, teacher, family member—whom they could trust and who, they felt, honestly cared. Through this relationship the children were able to learn to trust adults and to see themselves as persons worthy of being loved and cared for. The road to health for sexually abused children is that simple and that complex.

As professionals concerned with the adoption of special-needs children, we believe in the importance of placing sexually abused children in families where they will be loved. Since sexual abuse is the ultimate betrayal of the parent-child relationship, the primary therapeutic resource available to sexually abused children is understanding, committed parents who can prove to them that parents can be trusted. The damage to the children occurred within families, and families are the best place for children to learn that parents do love, care for, and protect children, and that they themselves are worthwhile human beings. Many sexually abusing families are too dysfunctional for the children to remain in or return to their family of origin.

Adoption is not a panacea, however; problems do not automatically disappear with placement. Adoptive placement often brings out many behaviors the children never exhibited in their own home or in their foster home, behaviors such as sexual acting out, anger and hostility, and open rejection of the adoptive parents. But most adoptive families willing to accept the challenge of special-needs children can successfully parent sexually abused children. For these families to do so, three things must be provided by the agency: (1) comprehensive training regarding the dynamics of sexual abuse, the needs of sexually abused children in adoption, and parenting skills for the adoptive parents; (2) complete information about the particular child's background and behavior, including the specifics of the sexual abuse and the child's emotional and behavioral reactions to it; and (3) continuing support services to the child and adoptive family after placement.

Most sexually abused children can adapt to a healthy adoptive family system and can learn to accept the sexual abuse as a part of their past, but a part that does not have to determine their future. Parents who are caring, committed, and able to communicate with the child can be the determining factor.

The Training Manual

Using the Manual: Notes from the Authors

This manual derives from a program of training adoptive parents to accept, understand, and parent sexually abused children that was begun in 1983. It has been revised and updated many times since then to reflect new research, the authors' experience, and the experiences of the families and children involved. It cannot be the last word on the subject and should be considered a guide to be adapted to the personal styles, needs, and expertise of those who use it. The following suggestions for using the manual and conducting the training are offered in this spirit.

Group Leaders

Two persons should act as coleaders of the training sessions. They can both be adoption specialists with the adoption agency, or one adoption specialist can work with experienced adoptive parents who have successfully parented sexually abused children. If an adoptive parent is available who has good group skills as well as a thorough knowledge of sexual abuse, the personal experience and expertise he or she brings to the group is invaluable. Additionally, a successful adoptive parent carries conviction to the group participants that they too can succeed in parenting sexually abused children.

Knowledge and Skills

The group leaders must be thoroughly knowledgeable in three areas: special-needs adoption; sexual abuse; and the use of the group method in preparing adoptive families. All sexually abused children should automatically be considered special-needs children, and the leaders must be knowledgeable about the effects of a special-needs adoption on the family system so they can assist the families in recognizing which issues relate to the sexual abuse and which are common to all special-needs placements. The leaders must also be thoroughly familiar with all phases of work with the sexually abused child. This includes a thorough knowledge of local and state laws, investigation methods and procedures, dynamics of the sexually abusing family, treatment modalities for the abusing family, impact of sexual abuse on the child, and treatment modalities for the child. The leaders should also be thoroughly familiar with all local therapeutic resources, their areas of expertise, and their success in working with sexual abuse victims. Finally, the leaders should be comfortable using group sessions as a training method. The use of the group method is an important aspect of the training process, for it enables the participants to identify with other adoptive families, removes the anxiety often present in one-on-one training, and allows the leaders to assess the participants' ability to deal with the issues associated with parenting sexually abused children through group or "norm" comparison.

The principal personal characteristics required in effective group leaders are: (*1*) acceptance of their own sexuality; (*2*) ability to talk about human sexuality and sexual practices; and (*3*) resolution of any personal feelings about sexual abuse. Since it helps to routinely begin training workshops by informing the participants that it is impossible to talk about sexual abuse without talking about sex and human sexuality, and since the ability to openly discuss sexual issues with children is one of the main skills the parents should cultivate, the group leaders must be capable of role modeling this behavior for the group. Yet this ability to openly discuss sexual issues is the most difficult skill for most of us to master because of lifelong prohibitions from our families and society at large. The leaders must be able to give themselves permission to use the "forbidden" words in the group. (Fortunately, this gets easier the more one practices.) To achieve this, the leaders must be comfortable with themselves as sexual beings and must also have resolved feelings generated by a personal history involving sexual abuse. Although the group dynamics and issues discussed invite personal disclosure from both the leaders and the participants, it must be remembered that this is group training, not group therapy.

Of course, many participants who were themselves victims as children have reported therapeutic effects from the training session. This may be the first time anyone has ever given them permission to talk about what happened to them, the first time they ever began to understand why they were victimized and the dynamics of their family system, the first time anyone ever told them that what happened to them was not their fault, and the first time they began to understand the effects of the abuse on their lives—the feelings they have, the choices they have made. Maintaining the balance between empathy for the adult victim and encouraging openness yet maintaining control of the group process requires objectivity as well as good group-leading skills. The leader who has not resolved her or his own feelings about sexual abuse cannot maintain the separateness required to lead the group.

Group Participants

Although research reports that the easiest groups to work with are those where the participants are more similar than different in terms of age, race, sex, and socio-economic status, these factors do not seem to greatly affect the development of group identity during workshops, for two reasons: (*1*) the participants all have a common goal in adoption; and (*2*) all share a common interest in the subject matter. Sex seems to be a great leveler, and by the end of the desensitization exercises, during which the participants are given permission to talk about sex and examine their own attitudes toward sex and sexuality, many of the more artificial barriers to group cohesiveness have been broken down. This then allows the group members to become involved in the common goal of learning how to parent sexually abused children.

The training should be provided before placement of a child with the family; if this is not possible, however, the family should be given the information on an individual basis before placement and scheduled for a training session as soon as possible. It is definitely preferable, however, to include the training as a part of the initial training required for all prospective adoptive families (other than newborn infant adoptors) rather than require it only for those families who are going to receive a child with a known sexual abuse background. The reasons are twofold: First, for more than half the children we have placed, the sexual abuse history was not confirmed until after adoption placement. Second, one of the purposes of the training is to help families understand that they can successfully parent sexually abused children. Many people are fearful of parenting these children because of lack of understanding; after training, almost all of the families have proved to be accepting of sexually abused children. This obviously increases the placement possibilities for waiting children.

Nuts and Bolts

The optimum group size is ten to 16 participants. This size allows for good discussion and participation by all members and enables the leaders to assess individual reactions to the material. The training is limited to adult family members because of the subject matter and the inhibiting influence of children on the discussions. If at all possible, all adults living in the home should attend the training, and we have included at times extended family members who will be involved with the child.

The preferred seating arrangement is around tables where all participants can see one another. Tables are needed because of writing assignments, and this seating arrangement promotes discussion and interaction. A large name plate of some kind for each person's first name should be provided, along with paper and pencils. Handouts can be passed out during the training session or collated and prepared in packets before the training.

The training is denoted as a one-day, six-hour workshop. When the same material was presented in two three-hour sessions, no difference was found in understanding or retention of information, or response to the material.

It should be noted here that our experimental efforts to shorten the training time have not been successful because they required leaving out information essential to understanding the dynamics of sexual abuse and learning the necessary parenting skills. Some others who have used this material report that they were able to shorten the training time considerably by leaving out the desensitization exercises. This is a grave mistake, for the reasons cited above in the "Group Leaders" section; indeed, those who have left this portion of the material out have acknowledged that they are uncomfortable talking about sexual issues. Without question, this is a tremendous disservice to the adoptive families and the children. Also, time is required to allow the participants to become comfortable about discussing the issues if they are to be able to move on to accepting the responsibility of helping the child.

The following materials are required for conducting the training session:

1. Blackboard or flip chart/chalk or pens
2. Pencils and paper for all participants.
3. Name tags
4. Handouts
5. For the secrecy exercise: paper, pencils, envelopes

To promote the comfortable atmosphere essential for this training, coffee, soft drinks, and snacks for the group should be available in the training room, and the participants encouraged to help themselves at any time. This allows each participant to maintain optimum personal comfort and the opportunity to literally "walk off" the anxiety some may feel when the more difficult issues are discussed. Many adult sexual abuse victims in the group head for the refreshment table when their identification with the issues becomes too painful; this permits them to regain control while still remaining in the room. This also holds true for those who have more difficulty discussing issues associated with sexuality because of their personal upbringing. If the refreshments cannot be in the training room, they should be easily available nearby during the formal breaks.

Notes to the Group Leaders

Those who use this manual should familiarize themselves with its ideas and concepts and then present the material in their own words and style—especially so when sex and sexuality are being discussed. Note also that this manual was not meant to be read to a group or presented verbatim. For this training to be successful, the group members must be involved in the process, and reading the material allows the group members to become inactive and disengaged. This can prove fatal for a group process in which the issues associated with sexual abuse are discussed, because denial can be so strong.

Users of the training manual will notice that no case examples have been provided in the training manual material—not even in those places where trainers are instructed to give an example. This seems unfair since case examples are extremely important in "personalizing" the training and helping the participants understand that we are discussing real children and real families—children and families whom we know. This is the reason, however, that examples are not given. For you to be effective and credible, you must talk about those children and families whom you know. Another benefit of using as case examples people whom you know is that these may well be the same persons who can serve as resources and support for families currently in the workshop. Although your case examples are not identified by name, when a "new" family experiences problems with a sexually abused child in placement, the most effective support they can have is another family who has "lived through it." It is much easier to establish these contacts if you are able to say, "Remember, this is the family I talked about who ..."

The foregoing advice is presented so emphatically because it emerges from the authors' own experience and from that of others who make these mistakes in using the training material, and then wonder why the group process is not going well.

Just One More Note

Because sexual abuse affects both boys and girls, and because adoptive parents are both men and women, we have chosen not to use a single "universal" pronoun, but instead, refer to the victims sometimes as "he" and sometimes as "she." This is done purposefully to reinforce that both boys and girls are victimized, and it can be too easy to fall into the trap of ignoring the number of male victims.

I. Group Introduction

A. Welcoming of the group participants to the training.

B. Introduction of the group leaders.

   1. Discuss experience with child placement/adoption.
   2. Discuss experience with sexually abused children.

C. Introduction of group participants.

   1. Personal information
      a) Age, marital status, residence, work information.
      b) Leaders encourage additional self-disclosure by asking pertinent questions about information provided.
   2. Information regarding current extent of their knowledge regarding sexual abuse of children, and where they received the information they have.

D. Explanation of rules regarding smoking, breaks, location and availability of refreshments, restrooms, and so forth.

II. Introduction to Understanding Sexual Abuse

A. Disclaimer.

Tell the participants that we have found that it is impossible to talk about sexual abuse without talking about sex, because child sexual abuse is about using children to meet adult needs, including sexual needs. Explain that we will therefore be discussing sex and sexuality openly and frankly, and many of the participants may be initially uncomfortable because we have been taught that sex is not something people talk about in public—especially not in mixed groups. Tell the participants that it is normal for them to be uncomfortable at first, and part of the purpose of the training is to help them feel more comfortable talking about sex because sexually abused children need parents who can talk to them.

B. Outline of the training.

Tell the participants that the training breaks down into three sections:

1. Talking about sexual abuse and talking about sex.
2. Understanding why sexual abuse occurs (dynamics) and its impact on the child victim.
3. Parenting the sexually abused child.

C. Tell the participants that there are three primary reasons why we have difficulty understanding child sexual abuse.

1. Denial—before we can attempt to understand sexual abuse, we first have to admit that it does happen—with alarming frequency—and that it does happen here.
2. Constraints regarding sex and sexuality—for us to be able to see or hear about sexual abuse, we first have to be comfortable with ourselves as sexual beings. We have to accept our own sexuality and the sexuality of our children, and many of us—perhaps most of us—are not comfortable with this. We are especially not comfortable discussing it. To become more comfortable with our sexuality, we have to examine and many times cast aside our moral, religious, and personal prohibitions regarding talking about sexual issues. This is a difficult thing for us to do.
3. Fears and myths about sexual abuse—it is easier for us to believe the fears and myths that abound about sexual abuse rather than deal with the reality of sexual abuse. We want to believe that sexual abuse perpetrators are strangers, not our neighbors or family members. We believe that because sexual abuse is so terrible, a child can never overcome it, and that relieves us of the responsibility to help the child.

III. Definitions and Statistics

A. Definition 1: Anything sexual with a child where the intent is to control or sexually arouse someone.

1. One of the team leaders should write the definition on the board.
2. Identify this as a definition widely accepted by social work professionals, but acknowledge that one of the problems professionals have on a national scale is that there are many different definitions of sexual abuse.
3. Ask the participants to list some activities/behaviors that would be considered sexual abuse of a child according to the above definition. Be sure the following are included:
   a) Looking at a child
   b) Inappropriate ways of talking to children about sex and sexuality
   c) Inappropriate touch, especially in genital areas or girls' breasts (fondling)
   d) Kissing in an adult manner
   e) Oral sex, anal sex
   f) Sexual intercourse
   g) Taking pictures/child pornography
4. Invite the participants to discuss why each of these activities would constitute sexual abuse.

B. Definition 2: Sexual abuse is a betrayal of trust involving overt or covert sexual actions—direct or indirect, verbal or physical—between a child and a trusted adult and/or authority figure.

1. Write this definition on the board with Definition 1, and explain that it comes from Voices in Action, a self-help group of adult victims.
2. Ask the participants to list some activities/behaviors that, according to this definition, would be considered sexual abuse of a child.
   a) Are the same behaviors listed?
   b) What new behaviors, if any, would the participants add?

C. Ask the participants to compare the two definitions and identify the similarities and differences. Include the following:

1. Both definitions include a broad range of activities and behaviors.
2. Definition 1 seems to focus on sexual behaviors, and it includes the more legal aspects of intent and motivation.
3. Definition 2 includes the more emotional aspects of sexual abuse and its impact on the child and focuses on the betrayal of trust that is inherent in child sexual abuse.
4. Tell the participants that they will need to be concerned with the

issues raised by both definitions: the actual behaviors (what happened to the child), how powerless was the child, what was the relationship between the child and the perpetrator, and what was the effect of the sexual abuse on the child.

5. Tell the participants that sexual abuse is the ultimate betrayal of the parent-child relationship, because parents uses their emotional power over their children to rob them of their childhood and force them into an adult relationship for which they are not psychologically, emotionally, or physically prepared. As a result of sexual abuse, the child learns that adults—parents—cannot be trusted. It is our task to help these children learn that there are adults in this world who will protect and care for them, that there are adults—parents—who can be trusted.
6. Tell the participants that this is the reason that families—parents—are the most important therapeutic resource available to sexually abused children: children can most successfully rediscover childhood and reexperience the childhood they did not have as part of a family; learning that parents can be trusted demands a continuing relationship between parents and child.

D. Statistical information

1. Tell the participants that one of the problems in treating sexual abuse is that good statistics about the actual number of victims are not available, partly because of differences in definitions and partly because sexual abuse is seldom reported.
2. Do tell the participants, however, that the following statistics are generally accepted:
    a) The Kinsey Report found that 26% of the adult women interviewed as a part of their study of the sexual habits and backgrounds of contemporary Americans had been sexually abused before the age of 13. This statistic has been confirmed by additional research, and professionals now state with certainty that fully 26% of all women in this country have a history of some type of sexual abuse.
    b) Research has indicated that at least 20% of all males in this country have a history of some type of sexual abuse. The most recent research indicates that the number for males may actually be higher than that for females.
    c) Based on these statistics, point out that 26% of the women and at least 20% of the men in the group are sexual abuse victims.
    d) Report that Kinsey found that only 6% of the women in their study who had been sexually abused had ever told anyone, so there is a good chance that the victims in the group have never discussed their victimization. State: "We will talk more about why people do not tell about their sexual victimization. How-

ever, I want to tell each of you who were victims—and you know who you are—that you were not responsible for what happened to you. You were a child, and as a child you could not give consent. It was not your fault. You were not responsible." The group leader should also tell the group that, if we were not working within a time frame now, we could talk about what happened to those persons in the group who were victimized because sexual abuse is okay to talk about. Encourage those who were victimized to talk about what happened to them, reinforcing that it was not their fault, and let them know that you will be available after the session or by appointment to discuss this.

e) Tell the participants that one out of ten children will be reported victims of sexual abuse this year.

f) Our statistics show that 86% of the children in foster care and 85% of the children we have placed into adoption since 1983 have a history of some type of sexual abuse.

g) In approximately 95% of the cases of sexual abuse, the perpetrator is known to the child, and in 72% to 85% of the cases the perpetrator is a family member. In only 5% of the cases is the perpetrator a stranger.

IV. Why Isn't Sexual Abuse Reported?

A. Secrecy exercise.

1. One of the team leaders should pass out paper and an envelope to each participant.
2. Instruct each participant to write on the paper an intimate secret. This should be something that is personal, perhaps something that they have never told anyone or only their spouse or most trusted friends. Do not provide additional directions or information. After all have written their secrets, instruct them to seal the paper in the envelope, write their names on the outside, and lay the envelopes on the table in front of them.

B. Tell the participants that there are reasons why children do not reveal sexual abuse. Discuss each of the following:

1. Sexual abuse occurs in private; there are usually no witnesses.
2. Sexual abuse is often the family's most closely guarded secret.
3. Children are not given permission to talk about sexual matters to adults.
4. The victim fears that she will not be believed (frequently reinforced by the perpetrator).
5. The victim fears retribution (also frequently reinforced by the perpetrator).
6. The victim fears the family will be broken up (the perpetrator will be jailed or she will be taken away, one or both of which frequently does occur).

C. Tell the participants that we do not want to believe that sexual abuse actually happens. We prefer to believe the myths about sexual abuse. Discuss the following myths:

1. Sexual abuse doesn't happen—at least not here.

   Sexual abuse occurs in all types of communities, in all types of neighborhoods, at all socioeconomic levels.
2. The child is seductive.

   A child is never seductive. She may have learned to respond to adults in a sexual manner, but this is a behavior learned as a result of sexual abuse.
3. It happens only to girls.

   As we have seen through statistics, males are at least as frequently—if not more so—victimized as girls. However, we still do not routinely talk to boys about sexual abuse and self protection.
4. Myths related to perpetrators.

   a) Only men sexually abuse children.

   b) Strangers are more dangerous to children.
   c) Homosexuals are more likely to be perpetrators than heterosexuals.

5. Freudian theory.

   Point out that orthodox Freudian theory rejects the reality of sexual abuse and substitutes the theory that this is the child's fantasy (oedipal complex, penis envy, etc.). These psychotherapists often perpetuate the denial and repressions of the sexual abuse experience.

V. Talking About Sex

A. Exercise in social learning about sex.

1. Give each participant a piece of paper.
2. Ask each participant to write down how she or he first learned about sex.
3. Initiate the discussion about learning about sex by asking several persons to share what they wrote.
   a) Expect some to say that they learned from peers, older siblings, books, parents.
   b) Ask the participants to discuss what the messages were in their families about sex. What spoken or unspoken messages were given to the children in the family about sex? Expect such responses as "We weren't supposed to talk about it." "Something about it was bad or nasty." "Sex is okay after you're married." "It was just a big mystery."
   c) Were the messages different for the boys and the girls in the family? If so, what were the differences?

B. Ask the participants how they have carried these messages with them into adulthood. If their attitude has changed, or if their messages to their children are different, how difficult was it to overcome the messages of childhood?

C. Ask the participants to discuss how they would want their children to view sex. Are the messages they are conveying to their children consistent with this?

D. Desensitization exercise.

(This is one of the most important exercises of the workshop. The purpose is to give permission to the participants to overcome their social restraints about talking about sex. To achieve this, the leaders must be comfortable discussing sex and using sexual terms, and must be able to convey this to the participants. The leaders must convey acceptance and encouragement, and must positively reinforce those who participate. Additionally, the leaders should encourage competition among the participants to see who can list the most terms. The leader should be prepared to add terms to initiate the listings or to keep the participants involved.)

1. Explain to the participants that talking about sex, especially to children, is difficult for most of us. This is especially difficult since few children have been taught the correct anatomical name for body parts. As adults, we prefer using the scientific names for body parts, since that is one way that we can remain uninvolved. Sexually abused children, especially, use the words they have heard and been taught, and since talking to the child about what happened to him or

her is very important, we must be able to use the words that the child uses. Tell the participants that the purpose of this exercise is to practice talking about sex and using the words that the child will use. Recognize that this exercise may be difficult for some, but tell the participants you want them to "forget" they were ever told that talking about sex was dirty or nasty. Tell the participants that talking about sex can be fun, and many people have found this to be one of their favorite parts of the workshop.

2. One of the leaders should write across the board the words "penis," "vagina," and "intercourse."
   a) Ask the participants to list all the words they can think of for "penis." Encourage slang, street, and childhood terms. As the terms are called out, list each under "penis." Make sure at least all of the most obvious terms are included.
   b) Repeat the exercise for "vagina."
   c) Repeat the exercise for "intercourse."
3. Note that most of the slang terms used denote aggression. Note that most of these terms are male terms and dehumanize the female and the sex act. This allows many men to distance themselves from their partner and from the act.
4. Note that many of the childhood terms denote playing games or animals (i.e., "pussy," "kitty," "cat and mouse"). Point out that many perpetrators use these terms, especially with young children, because it reinforces the "play" aspect of the sexual abuse and reduces the likelihood that the child will tell.
5. Point out that when children talk about what happened to them they will use words they know, which will usually be slang or childhood terms. Tell the participants that it is extremely important to allow children to use the words they know (remind them of the messages we convey when we tell a child that the words are dirty or nasty).

E. Explain to the participants that children will talk only so long as they feel that they are being believed and that what they are saying is being accepted, and professionals agree that the most important part of the healing process for the sexually abused child is being able to talk about what happened.

1. Tell the participants that our research has shown that more than one-half of the children we placed into adoption since 1983 had not discussed the previous sexual abuse with anyone before they went into adoption. Explain that there are several reasons for this, but the most important is that in adoption the child finally feels protected from the abuser and begins to establish a trust relationship with a parent. For this reason, the adoptive parents may be the first people to hear about the sexual abuse, and their reactions will determine how much the child tells and how they feel about themselves.

2. Tell the participants that as difficult as it may be to hear the child they love talk about their victimization, they must be able to control their emotions and remain calm. This will encourage the child to continue to trust and confide in them, which is the basis for a healthy parent-child relationship.
3. Tell the participants that if they reach a point where they cannot control their feelings, they should excuse themselves after reassuring the child that she or he did absolutely nothing wrong, that the sexual abuse was not their fault, and that they are sorry that the child had to suffer in that way. The parents should also tell the child that it makes them very sad and very angry that their child was hurt in this way. Tell the child that you want to hear more about it, but right now you need some time to think about what the child said. Thank the child for trusting you enough to tell you, and verbally and physically reassure the child that with you and in your home he is safe and will not be hurt that way again.
4. Explain to the participants that we have found that this kind of communication is essential to being therapeutic. We have found that most adoptive parents who had thought this would be impossible for them to do discovered that they did have the strength when it was their child who had been hurt and their child who needed them. When the parent becomes the child's confidant concerning the sexual abuse, and when the parent uses this opportunity to demonstrate that there is nothing the child cannot tell the parent, the parent-child relationship becomes stronger. When parents assure the child that he is safe and protected, they are telling the child that in this household the parents do fulfill their promises to children: parents do love, care for, and protect children.

VI. Dynamics of Sexual Abuse

A. Introduction.

Tell the participants that to help the child we have to understand how and why sexual abuse occurs. Emphasize that helping children overcome the effects of sexual abuse is not difficult as long as we are willing to accept that it happens—and that it happened to your child.

B. Family assessment model.

1. One of the team leaders should diagram the Cohesion Scale of the Olsen Circumplex Model of family assessment on the board, as shown in figure 1. (For a complete description of the Circumplex Model, see *Family Processes* 25 [September 1986].)
2. Explain that this diagram is one way of looking at families and how they function. It is used because it is relatively simple to understand (and draw on the board) but it is also very helpful in identifying the difference between normal or healthy families and those families—like sexually abusing families—that are dysfunctional.

Figure 1. Circumplex Model

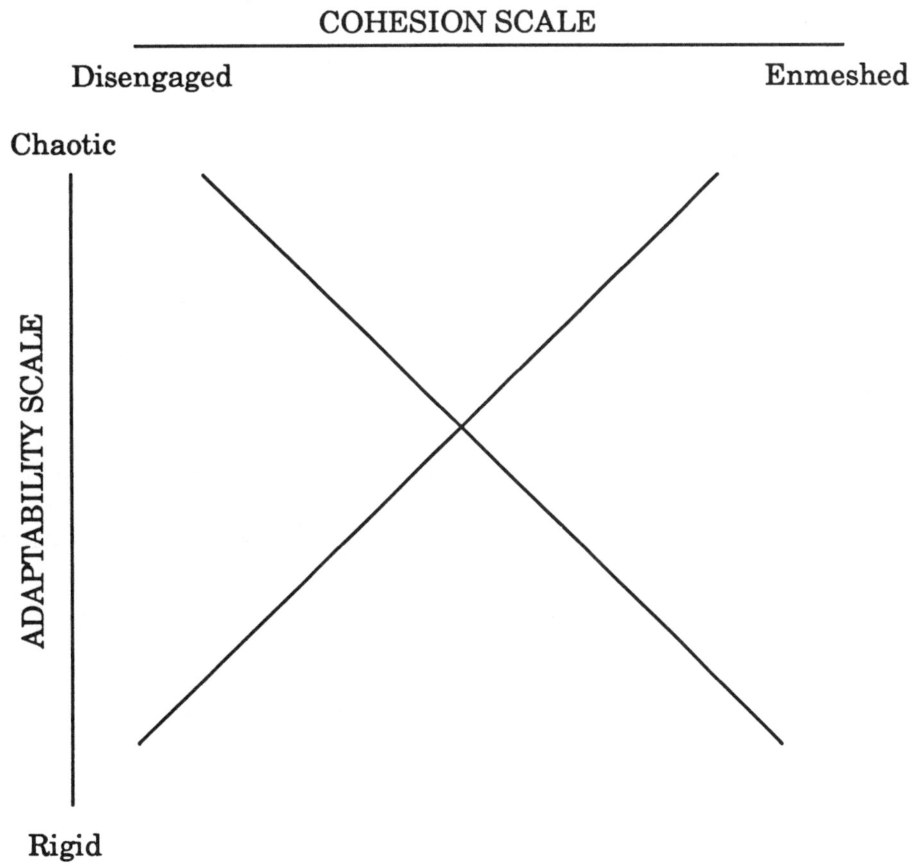

3. Explain the cohesion scale.
   a) Cohesion refers in this context to the degree of unity among the family members, how "together" the family members must be to feel safe and secure. It refers primarily to the emotional togetherness of the family as opposed to the physical togetherness, although many times the physical proximity of family members indicates the amount of family cohesion.
   b) Explain the identifying characteristics on the cohesion scale (give examples of the types of families). It generally helps to define the extremes first.
      (1) "Enmeshed" refers to the family unit that does not function unless all family members are in total agreement, working together for a common goal. The family members rarely, if ever, use "I," "me," or "mine"; rather, they say "we" and "our." The family does not tolerate any one member to separate from the family unit; and if one tries, all members of the family cooperate to bring the straying member back, using any psychological pressure necessary. If family members are successful at becoming independent, they are often cast out, disinherited, or no longer considered a member of the family. Often this family has many "family secrets," which the entire family cooperates in keeping hidden, and which serve the purpose of keeping the family unified. Oftentimes grown children do not leave home, or they establish their own homes nearby. Family members are in almost constant communication with one another, and they always know where all the other family members are at any given time.
      (2) "Disengaged" refers to the family that is the complete opposite of the enmeshed family: not only do the family members not know where the other members are, they usually don't care. Every member of the family is an individual, encouraged to do his own thing; and, unless the relationships are specified, it is difficult even to identify the persons as members of the same family. Individuals express themselves selfishly and seek gratification of individual needs, rather than considering the good of the family as a whole. There is little emotional bonding among family members. Family members rarely participate in family activities, rarely even eat a meal together. Every person in the family is supposed to be self-sufficient and responsible for meeting his or her own needs, and this includes the children in the family. Parents tend to see and treat the children as little adults rather than recognizing the special needs of childhood. Many affluent families and many "Yuppie" families tend to be disengaged.

4. Explain the adaptability scale.
   a) Adaptability refers to the family systems' response to outside events or the family's response to change.
   b) Explain the identifying characteristics of the adaptability scale (give examples of the types of families). Again, it helps to define the extremes.
      (1) "Rigid" refers to families whose members always live by the family rules, which are frequently not verbalized. The rules are generally autocratic, established by the dominant family member, usually the father. The family often deals harshly, oftentimes physically, with those members who disobey the family rules, so there is rarely any open show of disagreement or rebellion. The message of who is in charge of the family is clear, and expectations of behavior are specific. When threatened by situations or events outside the family, the family's reaction is to dig in their heels and become even less open and more reliant on maintaining family traditions and methods of operation. This family's frequent statement is "That's the way we've always done it and have gotten along just fine." Within the family unit, roles are specific and well defined, and family members are not allowed to step outside their assigned roles.
      (2) "Chaotic" refers to the family system that has no structure whatsoever. In this family, anything goes and there is no consistency of expectations, behaviors, or reactions. The family has no sense of family history or tradition, and the individual members often do not have strong internalized values of right and wrong. Chaotic families frequently create crises within and outside the family system, the use the crises to mask the family's lack of unity. The family members do not live within any assigned roles, and children may assume the parental role. These families are frequently not tied to any place, a job, or a home; or, conversely, the chaos may be reflected in emotional bonds among the family members with roles and expectations subject to change at any time.
5. Explain that families that operate in any of the extreme corners of the grid are dysfunctional families. There are therefore four types of dysfunctional families: *(1)* chaotic-disengaged; *(2)* chaotic-enmeshed; *(3)* rigid-disengaged; and *(4)* rigid-enmeshed. Families in these corners display the combined characteristics of the categories previously described.
6. Explain that healthy families function near the center of the grid, with some families operating more flexibly than others or more connected than others. In other words, in healthy families there is a

sense of family unit while individual members are encouraged to develop their own personalities, talents, and skills. Likewise, in healthy families a balance is achieved between structure and stability.

7. Indicate that families who operate in the more structured to rigid half of the grid are generally the more closed families, meaning that these families derive their primary support from within the family system and are not as concerned with or connected to the outside world. These families are not joiners and may not have many friends outside the family. Many healthy families are closed systems; they become dysfunctional, however, when they begin to disassociate themselves completely from the outside world and become isolated.
8. Point out that families who operate in the more flexible to chaotic half of the grid are generally the more random or erratic families, meaning that they are generally rather unpredictable in their behaviors and responses to stimuli. Again, many healthy families are at times unpredictable and interact continuously with the outside world; however, random families become dysfunctional when all their energies are concentrated on others and the outside world.
9. Explain that, by its nature, sexual abuse of children indicates that the child's family is dysfunctional; in fact, research shows that sexually abusing families are generally the most dysfunctional families.
10. Tell the participants that sexually abusing families add one other factor to the family dysfunction—sexual dysfunction. Within these dysfunctional family units, one or more adults view sex with children as an acceptable means of meeting sexual needs. Too often these adults were sexually abused as children, thus perpetuating the cycle on their own children. These people who had no one to turn to, no one to tell, no one to help them, act out their own victimization—creating more victims as they try to reconcile their anger with the world for not protecting them.

C. Types of sexual abuse in dysfunctional families.

1. Cite three types of sexual abuse: *(1)* rape of a child, *(2)* incest, and *(3)* systemic assault.
2. Use the family assessment model on the board to explain the types of sexual abuse and types of dysfunctional families that produce the different types of sexual abuse.
   a) Rape of a child.
      (1) Rape of a child refers to that type of sexual abuse that occurs in only 5% to 10% of all cases of sexual abuse, but is the most feared by parents when children are cautioned not to talk to strangers. Perpetrators may be either known to the child or a stranger, but no trust relationship exists between them;

therefore, the sexual abuse does not significantly damage the child's ability to trust parents. Fear of other adults may be the primary psychological effect, which can be relatively easy to overcome with parental support and established rape/trauma intervention techniques.

(2) Rape is usually violent and assaultive, with threats made toward the child or the child's family. No conditioning of the child takes place.

(3) Medical attention may be required because the assault may well cause physical injury to the child.

(4) Rape occurs in all types of families, but it is the least reported type of sexual abuse to child welfare agencies, for two reasons:

i) If the child is a member of a healthy family, the family responds positively to the needs of the child. This includes obtaining medical/psychological assistance as needed by the child and family, as well as reporting the assault to law enforcement and following through with prosecution of the offender.

ii) If the child is a member of a dysfunctional family, there are often other types of sexual abuse occurring within the family unit, which the family does not want called to the attention of the authorities. Rape of children may often be a characteristic of families who promote sexual abuse through systemic assault.

b) Incest.

(1) Incest refers to the traditional type of sexual abuse where the perpetrator is always a trusted person who is important in the child's life, usually a family member or close family friend. The trust relationship between child and perpetrator is of primary importance in incest. The child is conditioned over time by the perpetrator to accept the sexual abuse, and conditioning may begin very early. The other family members are generally aware of the incest and participate, either actively or passively, in promoting the incestuous behavior.

(2) Explain that incestuous families are rigid and enmeshed. Ask the group participants to identify those family characteristics of rigid/enmeshed families that would allow for and promote incest. Be sure the following characteristics are included:

i) Problems are kept within the family, including problems of sexual dysfunction that could lead to sexual abuse.

ii) Solutions to problems are believed to be found within the family.

iii) Enmeshed families limit contacts with those outside the family unit, promoting withdrawal and isolation.
iv) Enmeshed families protect other family members.
v) Enmeshed families protect family secrets.
vi) Secrecy of sexual abuse is maintained not only by perpetrator and victim, but if a family member does tell, the entire family mobilizes either to force a recantation or to force the family member out of the family—the ultimate punishment in an enmeshed family because the banished member cannot function without the group.
vii) The violence and authoritative characteristics of the rigid family also insure secrecy.
viii) Roles within the rigid family set up the victim and perpetuate the abuse. Usually role reversal occurs between victim and mother, with the victim assuming more and more of the wifely duties in maintaining the household.
ix) The dominating father/husband perpetuates the mother/wife in the passive, indecisive, childlike role.
x) The rigid family system resists any attempts to change the established roles and relationships within the family.

3) Explain that, because of these characteristics, incest is usually not reported by the victim or other family members until the roles are well established, especially since in the incestuous relationship the victim receives a special position in the family—lover, favored child, dominant female—and other family members are conditioned not to tell family secrets or involve those from the outside. When finally reported, the incest victim is the most difficult to treat because of these same characteristics. Although the victim may dislike the sexual abuse, she generally enjoys the special attention received because of the abuse. In addition, if the abuse and conditioning have continued for a long period of time, a lover relationship may be established that is confused with the parent-child relationship, so that the victim feels that she is only truly loved by the perpetrator.

C. Systemic assault.

(1) Explain that systemic assault is that type of sexual abuse in which the family systemically allows the children in the family to be sexually abused. The sexual abuse is often overt, where the parent actively participates in the sexual abuse, usually initiating the sexual conditioning during infancy.

Often one parent is absent from the family, usually the father. Victims of systemic assault frequently cannot remember when they were not being sexually abused, and often their earliest memories involve sexual activity. In these families, no protection is given children, and any adult near the child is a potential perpetrator. Victims often cannot remember all the persons who sexually abused them. Drug and/or alcohol abuse is common among the adults, and some form of prostitution by the parents is not uncommon. The prostitution often involves the children in one form or another. Sexual access to the children is often given in exchange for money or a commodity such as food, a place to stay, drugs, and so forth. Systemic assault frequently is found in families where extreme physical neglect and abuse are present. The family may have a long history of being reported to child welfare agencies for neglect and/or abuse, but these families are often highly transient, and confirming the reports and protecting the children are difficult. In most instances, these children are eventually removed from the family because of the physical neglect and abuse, and the sexual abuse is not revealed by the children until after the children feel safe in adoptive placement.

(2) Explain that families in which systemic assault occurs are chaotic-disengaged families. Ask the participants to identify the characteristics of the chaotic-disengaged family that would allow for and promote systemic assault. Be sure the following are included:

i) The parents in the disengaged family are primarily concerned with meeting their own needs, not the needs of the children.

ii) The parents have little emotional bonding to the child except as an extension of themselves.

iii) Because of the inability to recognize the specific needs of childhood, and the parents' consuming need for meeting their needs, they do not believe that the sexual abuse is harmful to the child.

iv) Prostituting or exchanging the child for commodities meets the parents' need and may enhance the parents' standing with peers.

v) In disengaged families, no one is looking out for the children's protection, so they are potential victims in all situations.

vi) The lack of protection in the disengaged family combines with the lack of structure in the chaotic family to make the children in the family vulnerable.

vii) The lack of internalized values regarding right and wrong opens the door to the sexual abuse of the children.

viii) The ongoing sexual victimization creates crisis, which the chaotic family requires.

ix) The lack of consistency regarding expectations keeps the child in a state of confusion, so values are difficult to establish.

x) The chaotic family, with no ties to any one location, finds it easy to simply move whenever threatened by outside situation or events (such as referrals to child welfare agencies).

(3) Explain that, because of the characteristics of the chaotic/disengaged family, sexual abuse is frequently not reported. The children have been sexually victimized since infancy, and they are school-aged and interacting with peers before they discover "everyone isn't doing that." By this time, their values are confused, but they feel ashamed of the abuse, believing they are somehow to blame. This type of sexual abuse often encompasses the more perverse types of abuse, which often adds to the shame. Also, since males are at least as frequently victimized as females, the myth of male sexuality adds to the boys not disclosing the abuse. In addition, the community is more concerned with the manifest signs of the neglect and abuse, and this is what is reported to child welfare agencies. Systemic assault victims may represent up to 75% of the older children available for adoption, but in only about 25% of these cases is the abuse known. Victims of systemic assault are the easiest of the sexual abuse victims to parent, providing that the structure, stability, and protection they missed earlier is combined with a strong sense of commitment and a great deal of patience.

VII. Secrets

A. Ask the participants to discuss how they have felt about the envelopes containing their secrets lying on the table during the previous discussions and exercises. Expect that most will indicate some anxiety, concern, or worry.

B. Have one of the team leaders take up all the envelopes. Do not tell participants that the envelopes will be returned.

C. Tell the participants that the envelopes will now be randomly distributed. Stress that the information inside the envelope is strictly confidential and no one is to open an envelope.

D. Redistribute the envelopes, making sure that no one gets his/her own envelope. Also make sure spouses do not get one another's envelope.

E. Remind participants they are responsible now for protecting someone else's secret. Remind participants they are not to open the envelopes. Tell them they are to protect the secrets as they would want others to protect their secrets.

* * * LUNCH BREAK * * *

VIII. Secrets (continued)

A. Return the secrets to their original owners.

B. Initiate a discussion of keeping secrets by asking the participants to respond to the following questions:

1. How did they feel when the team leader collected the secrets?
2. How did they feel when the secrets were randomly redistributed?
3. How did they feel during the break knowing that someone had their secret?
4. Did any participants take any steps to protect their secret? If so, what?
5. How did they feel about being responsible for keeping someone else's secret?

C. Relate the secrecy exercise to the child's maintaining the secret of having been sexual abused by asking the following questions:

1. What feelings would you expect a child keeping the secret of sexual abuse to have?
2. How would you expect a child keeping that secret to act?
3. What do you think a child would need in order to feel safe about telling the secret?
4. How would you expect the abusing family to react if the secret got out?
5. How do you think a child would feel after telling the secret to someone outside the family?
6. How could you get a child to tell the secret?

IX. Impact and Effects of Sexual Abuse

A. Effects on the child.

Tell the participants that two well-known researchers have identified four main ways in which sexual abuse affects a child.

1. Betrayal—Sexual abuse is the ultimate betrayal of the parent-child relationship. Even if a parent was not the perpetrator, the child perceives that the parents did not fulfill the promises inherent in parenthood of keeping the child safe from harm and nurturing the child. When a parent does participate in the abuse, the child feels doubly betrayed and develops a natural suspicion of parents and all adults.
2. Powerlessness—Sexual abuse teaches a child that she has no control over what happens to her. She does not even have control over her own body; it is subject to invasion at the whim of others. This lack of basic control and feeling of powerlessness frequently becomes so pervasive that the child is open to repeated victimization. She begins to develop the conviction that she cannot control what happens to her.
3. Stigmatization—Because sexual abuse does not happen to everyone, the child begins to recognize that he is different from other children. This feeling of being somehow different gradually becomes a feeling of shame, because he internalizes the idea that he is in some way responsible for the sexual abuse. This is compounded by the messages the victim received earlier from the perpetrator when he was repeatedly told that the abuse was his fault. Society's reaction to discussions of sex, and especially to deviant sex, reinforces the child's sense of shame and guilt.
4. Sexualization—Sexual abuse teaches children sexual behavior that is inappropriate for their age and developmental stage. They learn to respond to their world—and the people who inhabit it—sexually. Sexual abuse results in children becoming inappropriately sexualized, since sexual stimulation replaces more appropriate forms of touch such as cuddling and holding the child. Additionally, sexual abuse teaches the child that sex is about power and control, that the person who is in the power position can manipulate other people sexually.

B. Feelings associated with sexual abuse.

1. Anger—The sexually abused child has a high level of unfocused anger. This anger may be directed outward toward others or inward toward himself. The child often does not know why he is angry or at whom he is angry; in adoptive families, however, this anger is directed primarily toward the mother in the home.
2. Depression—Depression is frequently referred to as anger turned

inward. Most sexual abuse victims suffer from depression at some time. This is usually related to the victim's sense of powerlessness, when they feel "There's nothing I can do." Research indicates that the level of anger or the depth of the depression after placement is an indicator of the degree of sadness the child feels as a result of the sexual abuse and the loss of the biological family.

3. Shame—The sexual abuse victim feels dirty or bad for participating in the sexual abuse, especially if she has been made to feel that she in any way participated in the sexual activity or even if she allowed it to happen.
4. Guilt—The sexual abuse victim frequently believes that she was somehow responsible for the sexual abuse. This is frequently reinforced by the perpetrator. She may also feel responsible for the break-up of the family unit.
5. Confusion—The sexually abused child is confused about sex and sexuality, family roles and responsibilities, and male/female relationships. He is also confused about himself, where he fits in the family or a community, and whether or not he can ever be "normal."

C. Effects on the healthy family.

1. Point out to the participants that most healthy adoptive families fall within the center area of the family assessment grid. Since we all try to re-create our families—where we felt comfortable or at least knew the rules of survival—sexually abused children will try to re-create the dysfunctional families they knew. Discuss, using the family assessment model, how the incest victim will try to pull the healthy family toward the dysfunctional rigid-enmeshed corner and how the systemic assault victim will try to pull the family toward the chaotic-disengaged corner.
2. Explain that some of this pull may be unintentional. For example, the incest victim has had little experience in making decisions or offering opinions, so she resists doing this because of a lack of practice or a fear of the consequences. As a result, the new parents find themselves making even the most basic decisions for the child. Conversely, the systemic assault victim comes from a family where there was little or no supervision of the children, so he may be accustomed to making even major decisions, such as whether or not to go to school that day. The child therefore has difficulty comprehending why parents should care where he's going to or when he will return. These children will often simply walk out the door, and the parents will discover they do not know where their child is.
3. Emphasize that adoptive placement upsets the balance of relationships in the adoptive family simply by adding another person. All families go through a period of experiencing a disturbance in the family until the new balance can be achieved. Compare the family to

a mobile on which the individual family members are perfectly balanced. The addition of one or more new persons to the mobile will cause it to swing and sway wildly for a while as the various family members adjust; then the new balance is achieved.

4. Explain that this is what happens to all adoptive families after placement; the added factor of sexual abuse in the child's history does not mean that balance cannot be achieved again, only that more patience and commitment may be required.

X. Parenting Skills for Adoptive Parents of Sexually Abused Children

A. Tell the participants again that parenting sexually abused children is not difficult if the parents are willing to risk a part of themselves for the child. Sexually abused children present special challenges because they force us as adults to examine our own values, beliefs, and expectations. Emphasize that this is an opportunity for us to learn more about ourselves and an opportunity for personal growth. The people who are successful at parenting sexually abused children are those who are secure and confident in themselves as sexual human beings, who are willing to re-examine their values and beliefs, and who are able to communicate these to children. The group leader should express confidence that most of those in the group possess these qualities or they would not be willing to risk adoption of special-needs children.

B. Personal attitudes and abilities.

Tell the participants that certain personal attitudes and attributes are needed for those who parent sexually abused children. Write the following on the board or on a flip chart:

Those who parent sexually abused children must:

1. Be comfortable with their own sexuality.
2. Be comfortable with their marital relationship.
3. Be able to accept the child's history of sexual abuse.
4. Be able to discuss the child's history of sexual abuse with the child.
5. Be able to teach the child appropriate sexual behavior.
6. Be willing to slowly help the child accept the family's values and attitudes toward sex and sexuality.

Ask the participants to discuss each of the six statements and why parents of sexually abused children must have these abilities and attitudes. Be sure the following points are discussed:

1. If the parents cannot accept their own sexuality and themselves as sexual human beings, they will not be able to accept the child's sexual history or communicate with the child about sexuality.
2. The parents must be comfortable and secure in their marital relationship as this may be tested by the child.
3. The parents must be able to accept that the child was a victim and was not to blame for the abuse, even though the child admits to feeling pleasure from the abuse and to setting up situations for additional abuse. The parents must accept that their child already has an extensive history of sexual activity far beyond the experience of most children, possibly even beyond the experience of the parents themselves. The parents must accept that this has already happened to the child, and there is nothing they can do to erase the experience.

They must now be able to help the child understand how and why it happened and that it was not the child's fault; and to do this they must be able to talk openly with the child about the past.

4. The parents must be able to accept that there is no way that they can "desexualize" the child. What the parents can do is to introduce the child to their values regarding sex and sexuality and help the child learn age-appropriate sexual behavior.

Press the point that the parents must accept that the child did not learn the inappropriate behaviors and unacceptable attitudes overnight, and it will take time for the child to accept a new set of attitudes and behaviors. Also, in order to demonstrate for the child their values and attitudes, the parents must know what these are and be able to articulate them clearly. Additionally, in order to teach the child age-appropriate sexual behavior, the parents must *(1)* accept that children are also sexual beings and a normal part of growth and development is sexual; and *(2)* know what sexual behavior is appropriate at different ages.

C. Ability to differentiate between the child and the behavior.

Explain to the participants that one of the things they must be able to do is not identify the child with the behavior. They must remember that behavior is learned, and therefore can be unlearned. Behavior is learned slowly over time, however. They must be able to understand, finally, that any unacceptable acting-out behavior is not automatically or necessarily a reflection of them or their parenting ability. The parents must not expect a perfect child. They must be able to view the child as a separate human being, not as an extension of themselves. If they can accept the child as a separate person, then they can allow the child her own mistakes and help her learn from them. To achieve behavioral change, the parents must be able to do the following:

1. Always be the adult—Do not fall into the trap of allowing the child to reverse roles so that she becomes the adult. Because sexually abused children had no childhood, the adult/parent role can be very comfortable for them.
2. Understand the behavior and why it occurs—By understanding the child's history—the behaviors and values learned by the child from other parents—adoptive parents can successfully distance themselves from the unacceptable behavior. Also, this generates more empathy for the child as a victim.
3. Discuss the specific behavior with the child—The parents must be able to clearly state exactly what the unacceptable behavior is and why it is unacceptable, then clearly explain what behavior would have been acceptable in that situation. Most children desperately want to please their new parents, but they do not know what to do. Be specific and factual.

4. Have a long-term goal for change—The parents must remember that behavior does not change immediately, and so goals for major behavioral changes should be long-term. Remember that sexually abused children have been repeatedly betrayed by adults—especially parents—so initially they have no reason to believe anything the new parents say, and they will have to trust them before any major changes occur in behavior.

D. What is a family?

Sexually abused children come from dysfunctional families, so they have few realistic ideas about how typical families operate. Many sexually abused children report that they think normal families are like those on television; so on the one hand they expect their new family to be just as abusive and dangerous as their old family, and on the other hand they expect their new family to be just like those on popular television shows. They do not know that most families fall somewhere in between their old family and the television families. Certainly in few families are major family crises solved in 30 minutes. Since they do not know what an average family is, sexually abused children do not know how to act in a family, and this is the most important lesson the family teaches. Remind the participants that sexually abused children did not have parents who acted like parents, and they were not allowed to be children.

1. Family roles.
   a) On the board or flip chart write "Mother," "Father," and "Children." Ask the participants to list as many tasks and responsibilities for each as they can to describe what mothers, fathers, and children do in healthy families. Ask the participants to discuss why the tasks and responsibilities are different and why they are assigned to that particular role.
   b) After all the tasks and responsibilities are listed, group those for mother and father according to the following headings:
      (1) Nurturing.
      (2) Safety and protection.
      (3) Teaching.
      (4) Enforcing/discipline.
      (5) Providing.

Explain that most parental responsibilities fall in these five broad categories. Most experts agree that the one task of children is to grow up psychologically and physically healthy. (Be sure that under the children's heading things such as "play," "explore," and "learn" are included.")

   c) Explain that in sexually abusing families, these roles with their accompanying tasks and responsibilities are not present. The new family must be patient in helping the child learn what a family is and how it operates.

E. Parenting skills.

Explain that the following are specific skills useful and necessary for parenting sexually abused children.

1. Repetition—Never expect to tell the child one time and have him remember. New behaviors and expectations are learned slowly over time, and the parents must be prepared to repeat themselves frequently and explain the new expectations clearly.
2. Consistency—The parents must be able to be as consistent as possible. Remember that the child is learning a whole new way of being, thinking and acting, and the expectations must be consistent. The discipline for misbehavior must also be consistent.
3. Structure and stability—The parents must be able to provide structure for the child every day. This is a vital part of establishing trust between parents and child. It is especially important for children from systemic assault backgrounds since they have never experienced structure and stability. They will initially fight against it, but it is reassuring to know that dinner is always at 6:00 P.M. and that the family will be living in the same house two days in a row.
4. Supervision.

   Sexually abused children do not have the inner controls and coping skills of other children, so close supervision is both necessary and reassuring. Remember that these children were not allowed to develop normal coping skills as they grew up, and it will take time for them to incorporate the new family's value system. Close supervision, especially of adolescents, helps to prevent inappropriate sexual acting out and also provides the child with a face-saving excuse if he finds himself in a situation he cannot control. Sexually abused adolescents have reported the relief they felt in potentially damaging or dangerous situations when they could say, "I'm late getting home so I've got to go, or simply "My dad won't let me do that." Remember that these children have felt powerless to control their lives, and they continue to require outside controls until they develop self-confidence and adequate coping skills.
5. Discipline.

   Physical discipline is absolutely forbidden, not to say useless because many sexually abused children, in order to survive, have learned to disassociate themselves from physical pain and honestly "do not feel it." Therefore, alternative discipline appropriate to the child's age and development is required. Loss of privileges, time-out, or running laps are all effective. Never use as discipline the removal of a favored activity, or participation in a skill or group at which the child is accomplished, because the self-esteem of all sexually abused children needs constant support.

6. Family roles and rules.

   Due to the confusion that sexually abused children feel about family roles, the parents must be able to explain very clearly who does what and why in the family. This will have to be repeated often, saying "Mom does ..." or "Dad does ... ." This is especially important because of the role reversal these children have experienced, and parents find themselves repeating frequently, "No, that's Mom's job. Remember, we talked about ... ."

   Also, the parents must remember that the family rules that govern behavior and family functioning are new to the child, and these rules must be repeatedly stated and explained. (If you don't have a good reason for a rule, reexamine the rule.)

F. Low self-esteem and secondary behaviors.

One of the most important things adoptive parents must remember is that for years before the child entered their home he was given the message—both openly and very subtly—that he was a worthless human being and all of the bad things that happened, all the pain the child experienced, were his own fault. Sexual abuse denies the absolute right to privacy and control over one's body, and the child feels powerless, demeaned, and degraded. Before long, the child accepts this view of himself as "bad," "no good," "worthless." The child does not feel worthy of being loved, so he is unable to accept that anyone could love and value him for himself.

Without the chance to develop normal coping skills and defenses against the predominant view of himself as worthless and bad, the sexual abuse victim believes it wholeheartedly and often translates this into behavior that confirms it. This behavior may be antisocial in the form of lying, stealing, or cheating. The adoptive parents must recognize the child's behavior for what it is: the child's way of showing the world that he is a bad person, combined with the dysfunctional survival skills the child learned in the original family.

Assure the participants that the child's misbehavior cannot be tolerated and appropriate discipline must be used in a consistent manner. The following ways are the most effective means of eliminating the negative behaviors:

1. Positive reinforcement—Recognize and praise the child for everything positive he does. Find things to praise the child for every day. Research shows that positive reinforcement should be used at least eight times as often as negative reinforcement or discipline. Children want to please their parents; and like all of us, they respond quicker to praise and recognition than to negative reminders.
2. Provide opportunities for the child to achieve mastery and control. This means finding areas—schoolwork, sports, special talents or

skills—where the child can excel and succeed, even if the successes are small in the beginning. Recognize that the child will not feel that he can successfully compete against others and may not feel comfortable in team sports initially, so you may have to experiment to find a sport or talent for the child.

3. Because the child already believes he will fail, the parents will have to encourage and sometimes insist on the activities. Initially, noncompetitive activities or sports where the child's only purpose is mastery of the activity may be the most appropriate. After the child gains mastery, encourage slight competition. As he gains even more confidence, provide greater challenges. Remember, though, that for these children even small setbacks may be extremely discouraging, so constant encouragement and praise are necessary. Never belittle any attempt at mastery the child may make.

   The same holds true for allowing the child to gain self-confidence in small ways within the family. Allow him to feel in as much control of his daily life as possible. Because these children easily feel overwhelmed, give him a choice of perhaps two alternatives rather than endless possibilities. Too many choices may result in the child being unable to make any decision at all.

XI. Life Stages

A. Tell the participants that the issues associated with the previous abuse never completely go away. The child will never forget that—at one time in her life—she was victimized. With the assistance of committed, accepting parents, however, the sexual abuse does not have to determine the child's future. Although the fact of the sexual abuse will never be erased, its importance to the child can be diminished. Although the child will arrive at the point where she thinks about the sexual abuse as "something that happened to me when I was a kid," the parents should be aware that there will be specific times in the child's life when the issues will be important again and will need to be openly discussed.

B. Tell the participants that this is one of the reasons that we emphasize maintaining positive, open communication with the child about the sexual abuse. Without these continuing conversations, the child may not feel comfortable talking to the parents when she needs help in again resolving the issues of the sexual abuse in terms of her current development. Also, if the parents are aware that the sexual abuse issues are important at different life stages, they can offer support, encouragement, and understanding without the child having to ask. When children are experiencing life-stage crises related to their past history of sexual abuse, they may not understand their fears or their reactions. Having parents that understand and can explain the related issues, feelings, and behaviors can help victims understand and develop effective coping skills. Tell the participants that we know that the issues of the sexual abuse will be important during the following times in the child's life:

1. Puberty (10–13 years old).

   With the onset of the physical changes associated with puberty, the sexual abuse victim experiences again the early fears associated with the abuse. The child begins to develop sexually, and she fears that she will again be seen by others as sexually available. She may try to mask the changes in her body or deny that she is becoming sexually mature. Some girls may deny and try to hide the fact that they have begun menstruating. Boys and girls may suddenly refuse to dress out for physical education class, afraid that someone may notice the bodily changes. They may also cling desperately to the toys of childhood, such as dolls and stuffed animals, in the belief that they can delay their growing up. Parents must recognize that this conflict between wanting to stay a child and wanting to grow up is typical for all children in this developmental stage; for the sexual abuse victim, however, this conflict is more intense, and the child's response may be a fearful rejection of growing up and becoming a sexually mature adult.

   The parents must empathize with the child's fears, recognizing that the basis of the fear lies in the earlier sexual abuse. Now is the time for the parents to reemphasize that the child is safe and protected and to review the child's ability to protect himself.

2. Early adolescence (12–15 years).

   While the physical changes associated with puberty produce fear for the sexual abuse victim, the emotional turmoil of early adolescence results in confusion. When the sexual abuse victim realizes that she cannot stop her physical development, she must begin to confront the questions of "Who am I?" Where did I come from?" and "Who will I become?" The child in this phase of development also must begin to accept herself as a sexual being, and for the sexual abuse victim this is confusing. The child experiences the pleasurable feelings associated with sex through masturbation, but she is frightened by what this may mean. The victim's view of sex may still be negative, so she has difficulty resolving how something so bad can feel so good. The child may demonstrate this confusion with a swaggering, exaggerated sexuality one minute and a derisive remark about sex the next. The child may also begin masturbating frequently, sometimes at inappropriate times or in inappropriate places, in an almost fanatical fascination with her sexuality. Again, parents must recognize that this confusion is typical for all children at this developmental stage, but again the sexual abuse victim's reaction will be more intense.

   The parents must be able to communicate clearly to the child the "why" of sex, the reasons that sex feels good, and the role of sex in intimate, loving relationships. The child must have reassurance that her confusion is not atypical, and the parents should use this opportunity to reinforce for the child that she is not to blame for the earlier sexual abuse. The parents must be able to help the child work through her feelings of guilt about sex feeling pleasurable.

3. Late adolescence (14-19 years).

   This stage of the child's development is usually marked by emotional and physical separation from the parents. As any parents of a 16-year-old can attest, it is a period noted for apparently unprovoked outbursts of anger. For the sexual abuse victim, this anger is intensified by the existance of previous sexual abuse. Since anger directed toward the parents helps the child to complete the separation from the parents, the old anger toward the abusing parent usually resurfaces. The parents can generally recognize rather easily the behaviors associated with this secondary anger. It frequently takes the form of oppositional behavior, outright defiance, and testing of parental authority. The sexual abuse victim also frequently expresses the secondary anger by being derisive, by rejecting adoptive parents, and by distancing herself from any association with her past.

The parents must be able to assist the child in dealing with this anger by helping him to distinguish and focus it. It is during this period that the child will express real hatred of the abusive parents, and the adoptive parents must be careful not to be shocked by his vehemence. The parents must not feed into the child's anger toward the abusive parents, even though this may be tempting; rather, they should reinforce the child's right to be angry about what happened to him while helping the child to work through and understand the anger.

4. Early adulthood (18–24 years).

   The years of early adulthood are frequently marked by periods of depression for the sexual abuse victim. These are the years of preparing for and leaving home, and the old feelings of abandonment and rejection return. These are the years during which a person begins to make the choices that may well determine the rest of his life, and the sexual abuse victim may question whether he is "good enough" to master the world as an adult. The feelings associated with the poor self-esteem return, so that he may doubt whether he can compete with his peers in college or in a career. He may question whether he is capable of making good decisions for himself. The young adult is also frequently faced with decisions about marriage or a continuing relationship of some type. He wonders whether he is really good enough to be married, whether anyone would want him as a life partner if she knew about the early abuse, or whether he would ever dare have children for fear of perpetuating the cycle of abuse. This period is marked by indecisiveness, the inability to commit himself, and a feeling of being alone.

   The parents must be available to the child to assist him with these difficult life choices. They must also recognize that the young adult is reexperiencing the old feelings of self-doubt and must be able to help review what he has mastered and accomplished. They must be open to helping the young adult talk through his feelings, express his doubts and fears, and recognize the progress he has made in the intervening years since the abuse.

5. Adulthood (age 21 and up).

   This is the period of resolution of the feelings generated by the sexual abuse. The adult has worked through the feelings and is able to say "that was one of the things that happened to me when I was a child." She is able to put it in perspective and accept it as something that can never be undone, but she realizes that the sexual abuse does not determine the rest of her life. The adult feels in control of life and capable of making the decisions needed to live a satisfying and contributing life.

   The parents of the adult must recognize that, in time of crisis, their daughter or son may again experience some of the old feelings associated with the sexual abuse, especially those feelings of self-doubt, guilt, and anger. These feelings are usually transitory, however, and will usually pass rather quickly, especially if the adult victim's family recognizes the feelings and helps the victim once again perceive the basis of their intensity.

C. Ask the participants if they recognize the list of feelings the child will experience through adolescence and adulthood: fear, confusion, anger, depression, and resolution. Point out that these are the same feelings the victim experiences as a child; however, these same feelings coincide with the major tasks of adolescence—answering the questions, "Who am I?" "Where did I come from?" and "Who will I become?" For sexually abused children, working through these questions demands that they reexamine the earlier sexual abuse and begin to understand it. For many sexually abused children, this process, which is completed over the years as the child is developmentally able to cope with the questions and their answers, results in the ultimate healing. It is the parents' task to facilitate this process.

XII. Questions and Answers

Ask the participants for any questions they may have about the material presented. Answer all questions as fully and completely as possible.

XIII. Conclusion

A. Tell the participants that the workshop is completed, but you would like to take a few minutes for their informal response concerning how useful in general they felt the workshop had been, what they had found especially interesting or helpful, what had been upsetting or unsettling, and what had been confusing or vague. Respond appropriately to all observations or comments.

B. Use this brief time as a winding-down period for the participants in which they can collect their thoughts and begin preparing themselves mentally for the rest of their day.

C. Acknowledge that some of the material may have been upsetting, and the amount of it may have been overwhelming.

D. Thank each participant personally for attending and participating.

E. Invite the participants to call or contact you with additional comments or suggestions for improving the workshop after they have had time to relax and assimilate the material.

F. As you straighten out the room and gather training materials, make yourself available to the participants for personal conversation and questions. Allow additional time after the session for this, since usually several persons have concerns and questions they do not want to discuss in front of the group.

Background of the Training Program

Review of the Literature

Because it is generally recognized that many cases of sexual abuse are not reported, there is good reason to believe that the number of child victims is higher than the reports indicated. The actual number of children molested is unknown. In the late 1970s, a national survey reported 336,200 cases of confirmed child sexual abuse, but many cases were identified that were undocumented and intentionally ignored [Sarafino 1979].

As the helping professions and the legal system became aware of the increasing need to protect children from sexual assault, child protection laws began to broaden and include new emphasis on sexual abuse. Despite definition discrepancies and gaps in reporting, the literature agrees that at least one of every four children will be sexually abused by the age of 18 [Schultz 1977; Sgroi 1975; Forward and Buck 1979; Lanyon 1986; Bass 1983].

To cite an example, the number of known child sexual abuse victims in one state, Texas, increased 133% from 1981 to 1985. According to the Texas Council of Child Welfare Boards, one in four girls and one in five boys will be sexually abused before the age of 18, as reported in the Longview Morning Journal [1987: 8-A]. These statistics are based on confirmed reports of child sexual abuse, according to the Texas Department of Human Services Child Protective Services Program.

No national standard definition of child sexual abuse exists. In the literature, "incest", "sexual abuse," "molestation," and other similar terms are used to describe different and varied sex acts with children. Duehn [1984] offers the following comprehensive definition of sexual abuse: anything sexual with a child where the intent is to control and/or sexually arouse someone. This definition is accepted by many social work professionals and encompasses: (*1*) looking at a child in a sexual manner; (*2*) inappropriate ways of talking to a child about sex and sexuality; (*3*) inappropriate touch, especially in the genital and breast areas; (*4*) kissing in an adult manner; (*5*) oral and anal sex; (*6*) sexual intercourse; (*7*) taking pictures/child pornography; and (*8*) any other behavior that meets the criteria of the definition.

Regardless of the definition or the nature of the sexual act, sexual abuse involves issues of power and control. Burgess and Holstrom [1978: 85] state: "Victims are pressured into sexual activity by a person who stands in some power position over them—age and/or position of authority. ...Victims are incapable of consenting because of their level of cognitive or personality development." Groth [1978B: 16] describes sexual abuse of a child by an adult as "a complex and multidetermined act." He states that the sexual act with a child may be (for the adult perpetrator) an effort to compensate for feelings of inadequacy and to escape from the conflictual or intimidating relationships with adults to the safer, less threatening world of a child. Discussing an incestuous father's motivation, Forward and Buck [1979: 33] assert that "the aggressor rarely commits incest to satisfy purely sexual needs." They feel that sex with children is a vain attempt to satisfy a variety of unmet emotional needs—feelings of inadequacy, the need for tenderness and understanding, and possibly to revenge actual or perceived rejection from key female figures in the abuser's life. Cohen [1983] states that sexual abuse can be related to an unhealthy token need for warmth and nurturance. Forward and Buck [1979: 163] add that incest is generally the effect, not the cause of fragmented family relationships.

Experienced professionals report a cyclical pattern in regard to child sexual abuse. Lanyon [1986] found molesters had a greater frequency of sexual abuse as a child than the average person. Groth [1982: 138] found that the majority of the perpetrators with whom he worked had been sexually abused. Fowler et al. [1983: 97] state that 80% of the child molesters they studied had been sexually abused. Groth [1982: 138] explains that the former incest victim becomes an offender in a effort to resolve the unresolved sexual trauma he or she experienced as a child. Cohen [1983: 159] supports this: "Any traumatic experience in childhood which has not been worked through will linger with damaging effects until adulthood.

The majority of child victims of sexual abuse are not molested by strangers. Sgroi [1978a: xvi] reports that society, in an attempt to deny the magnitude of sexual abuse, assumes that "most cases involve perpetrators who are strangers to the child and who fit the mythical 'dirty old man in the alley' stereotype. ...Most child sexual abuse involved intrafamily perpetrators—fathers, stepfathers, uncles, mothers, boyfriends, etc.—people who have ready access to the child in his or her home." Conte and Beliner [1981] found that most molestation is done by men who are not strangers, but are known to the victim and are often related to the victim. Lanyon [1986] describes the typical molester as "most commonly a respectable, otherwise law-abiding person who may escape detection for exactly that reason." Forward and Buck [1979] describe the incestuous father as often being a "law-abiding, hard-working guy-next-door who somewhere along the line has lost the ability to control his impulses."

Because the abuser has a relationship with the child, has access to the child, and has a position of power and control in respect to the child, violence is seldom necessary. The work of Lanyon [1986] and Shultz [1977] reveals that 90% of all sexual offenses against children do not result in any violence or physical damage. It is not unusual for sexual abusers to use the pressure of psychological means, and the harm to the child is psychological rather than physical [Lanyon 1986]. Forward and Buck [1979: 21] include the absence of violence as one of the "recurring themes" of incest, stating, "When a father makes incestuous advances toward his daughter, he rarely resorts to force or violence—he has no need. There is a tremendous psychological coercion built into the father-daughter relationship." Groth [1978a] warns against basing a judgment about the occurrence of a sexual abuse on physical trauma. Sgroi remarks [1978b: xvi] that since child sexual abuse often involved nonviolent, nonforceable contact between the victim and the perpetrator, many cases are missed and many children remain unprotected.

Burgess and Holstrom [1978: 86] say that material rewards, social activities, adult approval, human contact and affection may be emotional controls used to instigate and ensure child cooperation. "The victim almost always participates in the incest voluntarily, not recognizing the subtle coercion that has taken place" [Forward and Buck 1978: 21]. Groth [1978b: 11, 12] describes two modes of operation for the sexual offender: (*1*) enticement, whereby he attempts to indoctrinate the child into sexuality through persuasion or cajolement, or (*2*) entrapment, in which advantage is taken of the child by putting the child in a situation in which he or she feels indebted and obligated. He says, "His aim is to gain sexual control of the child by developing a willing or consenting sexual relationship." When one acknowledges that physical damage to a child's genitals determines neither whether sexual abuse occurred nor the extent of psychological trauma the child suffered, other factors must be considered.

There is conflict in the literature regarding what causes the ongoing damage to the child. Some believe that sexual behavior between a child and a trusted adult is an attention-gratifying act that is not seen by the child as traumatic [Shultz 1977: 111; Forward and Buck 1979: 24]. These authors feel that the impact on society and its reaction cause the primary damage to the child. "The reaction of the family, society, and significant others has the ability to assess the amount of psychosocial aftereffects the child will suffer" [Shultz 1977: 114]. Others feel that the dynamics necessary for sexual abuse to occur (the secrecy, the emotional blackmail, the conflict of power and control, and role confusion) are what result in trauma for the child. Cohen [1983] states that sexual abuse results in a severe disruption of the sequence of personality development. She does concede, however, that the younger the child, the less the child will suffer psychological consequences, providing no physical trauma was done and that sufficient care and support were received.

Finkelhor and Browne [1985] feel that sexual abuse of a child is damaging to the child's physical and emotional development, but that the child's age, the psychological maneuvers, and the reaction and amount of support of the family play a major role in determining the extent of the child's trauma. The following are important factors:

1. *The relationship of the child and perpetrator.* Sgroi [1978a: 135] reports that "the greater the emotional distance between the child and the perpetrator, the less emotional trauma can be expected." She adds that the more violence, fear, and shame are involved, the more emotional trauma can be expected. She further notes that the more integrated the perpetrator is with the child's family, the more complicating are the effects of relationship, degree of trust, and possibility of family disruption. Bass [1983: 24] proposes a hierarchy of trust that can be used to assess a child's feeling of betrayal and devastation—the higher the perpetrator on the hierarchy, the greater the trauma: father is the top level; then grandfather, brother, and uncle; strangers are on the lowest level. "Children trust the adults in their lives, even when the adults are untrustworthy, because they have no choice. When that trust is betrayed, they learn the world is not dependable."

2. *Family reaction/support.* The amount of trauma a child suffers due to sexual abuse is usually related to the reaction of the family, which is related to the identity of the perpetrator. If the perpetrator is a control figure in the family, disruption and crisis will be more severe. When a family member is the perpetrator, the family will assess the gain and loss factors of supporting the child versus the perpetrator [Sgroi 1978a: 136]. Adams-Tucker [1982: 1255] reports that "children whose parents do not support, believe, and protect, are more seriously disturbed than ones who

have protective parents." Elwell [1979: 233] states, "The literature agrees that family reaction is especially significant and will influence the process of resolution for the child." When family standards conflict with societal standards, the long-term effects upon the child will be greater [Cohen 1983].

There is widespread agreement throughout the literature that sexual abuse has a profound effect on a child. Finkelhor and Browne [1985] suggest that sexual abuse produces conflict and confusion that can be separated into four trauma-producing dynamics. To assess the degree of trauma experienced by a victimized child, each of the four factors must be considered and explored:

1. *Traumatic sexualization.* The child's sexuality—sexual attitude and sexual feelings—are shaped in a developmentally inappropriate and interpersonally dysfunctional fashion as a result of sexual abuse.

2. *Betrayal.* The dynamic by which children discover that someone on whom they were vitally dependent has caused them harm.

3. *Powerlessness.* The process in which the child's will, desires, and sense of efficiency are continually contravened and disempowered.

4. *Stigmatization.* The negative connotations that are communicated to the child about the experience and that then become incorporated into the child's self-image.

Self-esteem of the child victim is seriously affected by sexual abuse. Characteristics of negative self-image—the feelings of inadequacy, immaturity, helplessness, and isolation—usually begin to form early in childhood and are present in the majority of sexual abuse victims [McCarty 1986]. Borgman [1984] reported that child victims often regard themselves as sex objects, as bad, isolated, and rejected, and they provoke rejection. Lee and Rosenthal [1983] found that child victims blame themselves for the abuse and describe themselves as worthless and bad.

Hoorwitz [1983] says that role confusion and lack of clear parental boundaries lead to the child's poor self-identity, and that the distrust of parent figures leaves the child with no strong ally or role model, increasing the child's poor self-esteem. Increasing awareness that social morals and family morals differ adds to the child's internalization of conflict and feelings of being worthless [Cohen 1983]. "The act of incest constitutes a violation of the child's right to a normal, healthy development and an abuse of her personal safety and boundaries."

Browne and Finkelhor [1986] report that a self-esteem inventory survey, conducted by random sample, indicated that women with a history of child sexual abuse were four times more likely to score in the "very poor" category than women who had no history of child sexual abuse; in their review of child sexual abuse victims, they found that 19% of child sexual abuse victims scored in the "very poor" inventory area of self-esteem. Sexual abuse conveys to children that adults cannot be trusted, and that children cannot protect themselves. For a sexually abused child, the world is an unsafe place.

In the last ten years the helping professions have placed special emphasis on child sexual abuse [Krenk 1984; Sgroi 1982]. The sexual revolution, strengthened child abuse laws, and specialized child protective programs were some of the factors that led to the disclosure of the widespread extent of sexual abuse of children and to the importance of helping them to understand what has happened, and of overcoming the resulting emotional damage. Forward and Buck [1979: 163] state, "Although sufficient damage has been done to her dignity and sense of self-worth, she does not have to be psychologically crippled for the rest of her life." Weinbach and Curtis [1986] say,

> The creation of a self-concept is a complex activity that grows out of many different interactions with the environment and persons who inhabit it. ... Regular incidents of abuse may not be sufficient in themselves to damage a self-concept if other life experiences are more positive.

They add that the development of self-concept continues throughout the experiences of every stage of life.

Timmons-Mitchell [1986] asserts that children with violent backgrounds need predictability and clear contingencies, as well as stable adult relationships that can withstand the child's expression of anger and aggression, and that can respond with forgiveness, giving the child hope. She says further that caregiving adults must emphasize the formation of positive relationships with others based on cooperation and trust, believing the child can learn quickly. Support, safety, and the positive role models the family gives to the sexual abuse victim are important in the healing process. Defining support as the "strength one person gives to another person in a stressful situation," Burgess and Holstrom [1978: 76] found that families who are able to be consistently supportive of the sexually abused child can take the lead in the counseling process, providing the direction for the child's recovery.

Finkelhor and Browne [1985] stress that the family's reaction to the child's sexual abuse has an impact on how affected the child will be. Research has shown that sexually abused children whose parents were not supportive and protective manifested more behavioral disturbances. Negative parental reactions aggravated the trauma for sexually abused children [Browne and Finkelhor 1986]. Borgman states that child victims need to be able to talk about the sexual abuse, "to relieve guilt and to gain allies within the family" [1984: 185]. He adds that a major need of sexually abused children is to develop more positive self-images through normal constructive interests and activities during day-to-day experiences. Lee and Rosenthal [1983] say that sexual abuse victims need support at home and people who will not overreact or overidentify with self-disclosure and the need to talk. Elwell [1989] stresses that the child victim's "strongest potential support system" is the family that is able to support, communicate, and reach out to the child's individual needs. Hoorwitz [1983] states that the family parenting an incest victim must be able to help the child understand human sexuality and the role of sex, as well as the power roles and limits of parents and children in a family unit. Cohen also says that an incest victim must be established in the kind of family relationship that can teach appropriate power and role boundaries [1983]. Supporting the claim that victims can and do recover from violent assault, Lee and Rosenthal [1983] remark that individuals survive and grow in the face of violent onslaughts, and this attests to the resiliency and tremendous strengths of human beings.

The sexual abuse problem is often deeply rooted and interpenetrating within a child's biological family. Providing protection for the child is vital, and "often the child is removed from the home" [Damon et al. 1987]; the multicausal problems that frequently exist within the sexually abusing family render the family unable to provide the protection, support, and nurturing the child needs. It is not surprising, therefore, that the number of sexually abused children in alternate care settings is high. Child welfare agencies responsible for these children are committed to the goal of providing an alternate family through adoption for those children unable to return to the biological family. Special-needs children in Texas are defined as children who are over the age of six, of a minority race, members of a sibling group, and children with physical, mental, or emotional handicaps [Shultz 1985]. Sexually abused children easily fit into the special-needs category because of their problems.

Research reveals that special-needs adoption can be successful, with adequate preparation of the family highlighted as one of the most important phases in the adoption process. As Nelson [1985: 34] states, "One of the most important contributions of workers to the placement process [of special-needs children] is to prepare [adoptive] parents for the adoption." She adds [85]; "It is hard to overstate the importance of thorough preparation [of the family] particularly to outright adopters who agree to adopt a child they barely know"; and in viewing reasons for adoption disruption, she found that, "receiving adequate information about the child increased the likelihood that the adoption would work out well, as did receiving adequate preparation of other kinds." Preparing a family for a special-needs child by sharing with them the child's history, in addition to providing special training to help the family understand the child's past, gives the parents insight and a true capacity to decide whether or not the child can be incorporated into their family. Nelson explains [1985: 86]: "The parents' own informed opinion about the suitability of a placement is one of the best predictors of outcome. ... The most effective preparation does not merely educate prospective parents; it enables them to take charge of placement decisions."

Knowing the child's past history and understanding how the past has affected the child enables adoptive parents to accept and to expect certain behavioral problems from the child. In studying unsuccessful adoptive placements, Festinger [1986: 39] found that the most frequent cause of disruption was the family's inability to cope with behaviors exhibited by the child. Barth et al. [1986] found that families that disrupted did not have sufficient information about the child: "Adoptions seem more successful in families whose parents expect and accept behavioral and emotional problems in response to the stresses the child has experienced." Katz states [1986]: "Successful adopters are stubborn and see the child's behavior for what it is, a desperate fear of the needed closeness. ... When they know it has nothing to do whatsoever with them as people, they can shrug off rejection and proceed with the nurturance they know the child needs." She adds that adoptive parents can be prepared by the agency for the child's past and behaviors: "The literature supports the use of groupwork with adoptive parents in the pre- and post-phase of older child adoptions." Barth et al. [1986] also says, "Adoptive parent group training sessions before placement help prepare parents for typical problems they will encounter with their child and help foster friendships with other adoptive parents who can support and understand them after placement."

To successfully work with and parent a sexual abuse victim, personal feelings and barriers must be explored. After finding that 68% of the girls and 50% of the boys at one treatment facility had been sexually abused, a program was begun to train staff members in helping the sexually abused child [Krenk 1980]. The program uncovered initial feelings (from the staff) of denial due to individual problems in dealing with sexuality and sexual abuse. The training enabled the staff members to "desensitize," thus decreasing extreme emotional reactions to child molestation and enabling them to place it in perspective with other problems; they were able to distinguish between normal behavior and behavior that is the result of sexual abuse.

The adoptive family can be the most important factor in a sexually abused child's healing process. To provide the support and guidance the child needs, a family has to be able to deal with the issues involved. To explain the development of the PET Program [Parent Effectiveness Training), Dr. Thomas Gordon reasoned that if professionals could be trained to communicate with children therapeutically, parents with an even greater desire to help their children could use these same tools and methods at home to the benefit of their children and the parent-child relationship [Jewett 1978: 58].

The family will also need to allow the child the opportunity to express and understand sexual abuse. To best do this, Burgess and Holstrom state that [1978: 78] the adoptive parents must come to terms with *(1)* their own feelings about the child's sexuality; *(2)* their own feelings about molestation; and *(3)* their own feelings about the child's rage. They add that the parents must be trained to deal with a person in a "sexual stress situation" by first being able to hear and deal with the situation personally; and second, by learning how to help the victim tell what happened [103]. They add that to help a child victim, "You must come to grips with your own feelings about sex. Being comfortable with one's own sexuality reduces the possibility of projecting values or prejudice onto the child" [102]. Elwell [1979] asserts: "Parents have to separate their own feelings and pain in order to be able to support and help the child." Cohen [1985] says that the family must realize the impact of sexual abuse on the child and understand the dynamics of sexual abuse, as well as the child's role as a participating victim. She also stresses the need for the family to believe the child and be able to talk with the child about the sexual abuse without any negative responses. Adams-Tucker [1983] says that adoptive parents need to be energetically supportive and strictly child-centered when their molested child talks about having been abused.

The challenge presented to the family that has adopted a child victim is best described by Katz [1986]: "The parents will use themselves daily, hourly, to accomplish what is the end goal of all therapy: To change the negative worldview of the child into 'I am lovable, competent, and have a safe place in the world'."

History of the Special Training

Since 1980, the Texas Department of Human Services in Northeast Texas has given particular attention to the adoptive placement of special-needs children—those who because of their age, race, sibling status, or handicapping condition are least likely to be adopted, and who, when they are adopted, require more effort from the adoptive parents to be incorporated successfully into the family system. As more of these children were placed with adoptive families, it became increasingly clear that another type of child should be added to the special-needs category: the sexual abuse victim.

The adoptive parents and the adoption specialists who worked with these families began to identify a set of characteristics and behaviors common to sexually abused children that the research indicated should be expected when dealing with victims of sexual abuse. Sexually abused children feel betrayed by the adults who abused them and/or did not provide the needed protection, so they have difficulty establishing trust relationships with the adoptive parents. Sexual abuse victims feel powerless in relationships, which may result in either extreme fear and anxiety or overcompensation by becoming overly controlling and domineering. They also feel different and usually see themselves as bad persons, and in adoptive placement will often act this out to counteract affection from the adoptive parents. Finally, they have been inappropriately sexualized and may continue inappropriate sexual behavior after adoptive placement.

These children presented multiple problems for the adoptive parents, with behaviors ranging from inappropriate sexual behavior (including sibling sexual abuse) to extreme rejection of the adoptive parents (including physical assault). The children also frequently had problems with peer relationships and in school performance.

To assist these families in maintaining the placements, intervention was required to help them understand the childrens' background of sexual abuse and its impact on their current behavior. It soon became apparent that the adoptive parents required more training and preparation before the placement of sexually abused children than was provided, and the agency began developing specialized training for adoptive families. Initially the training was provided individually for families who either already had sexually abused children in placement or who had been selected for a sexually abused child. It was soon clear that the main difference between those families who received the training and those who did not was one of attitude: the families who were prepared felt that they could successfully parent sexually abused children and, understanding where the behaviors originated and how they could help the child, were less likely to see the child as damaged or the placement as hopeless. Rather, they viewed the difficult behaviors resulting from the sexual abuse as challenges to be overcome on the road to health. The adoptive parents' energies were thus focused on repairing the damage done by the sexual abuse rather than agonizing over the trauma inflicted upon the children. The families were able to establish the structure necessary to help the children to begin to learn healthy coping skills and appropriate behavior.

By 1983, the agency was placing many special-needs children into adoption, several of whom had a known history of sexual abuse. For many of these special-needs children, however, the sexual abuse was suspected because of family dynamics and the behaviors of the children but the children had never acknowledged that they were victims. For these children, the disclosure of the sexual abuse came after adoptive placement, when the child felt safe and began to believe in the long-term commitment from the adoptive parents. It was recognized then that all adoptive families needed the information provided previously only to those who would be getting a known sexually abused child. The need for all adoptive families to be trained in parenting sexually abused children was confirmed when a review of the records of a local emergency shelter revealed that 86% of the children (158 out of a total of 184) who were removed from the biological family and placed in the emergency shelter during a four-year period from 1978 to 1981 had a history of sexual abuse. The agency, therefore, formalized the training and included it in the group preparation required for all prospective adoptive families.

Since 1979, group preparation for prospective adoptive families has been the primary method used by the adoption unit for preparing and assessing adoptive families. All adoptive families, except foster parents who had completed foster parent training and who were adopting children placed in their home, are required to attend these group sessions. This training includes helping the families understand *(1)* the dynamics of abuse and neglect; *(2)* the foster care system; (3) the respective roles of the agency, foster parents, and adoptive parents; *(4)* the impact of previous abuse/neglect, removal from the family of origin, foster care placement, and adoptive placement on the child; *(5)* the impact of adoption on the adoptive family system; *(6)* parenting and communication skills and discipline; *(7)* the legal system; and *(8)* the placement needs of special-needs children. This training is generally provided in six three-hour sessions.

Since the adoptive families were expecting to participate in group training, incorporating the session on parenting sexually abused children was relatively easy. The new material was presented in two three-hour sessions, lengthening the total group training to eight three-hour sessions, with the sessions on sexual abuse coming in as the fifth and sixth sessions, followed by the sessions on the impact of adoption on the family and the characteristics of special-needs children in adoption.

Since the beginning of the new training in 1983, it has been enriched by continuing experience in the adoptive placement of sexually abused children, as adoptive families and the children they parent have expressed new needs for information and understanding, and as new research has become available. Also, due to both time and fatigue, the two three-hour sessions were subtracted from the format and changed to a one-day workshop, with more flexibility in scheduling. The training on parenting the sexually abused child remains a requirement for all prospective adoptive families, whether it is presented in a one-day workshop or as a part of the group training sessions.

The Training Content

Families that indicated an interest in the adoption of special-needs children were included in the sexual abuse training and, in most cases, had completed the required group sessions for special-needs adoptions. The families had originally either contacted the agency expressing an interest in the adoption of a special-needs child or were recruited for a specific child.

The training outline was as follows:

A. Recognition of the problem (sexual abuse of children)
   1. Statistics
   2. Definitions

B. Aspects of denial
   1. Societal
   2. Personal attitudes and feelings

C. Desensitization
   1. Breaking the secrecy barrier
   2. Acknowledgment of the power of words

D. Dynamics
   1. Family assessment model
   2. Types of sexual abuse
   3. Role characteristics and effects

E. Impact of sexual abuse
   1. On the child
   2. On the family

F. Parenting skills
   1. Self-awareness
   2. Communication skills
   3. Specific parenting skills
      a. Family structure and role realignment
      b. Interactive restructuring

G. Life stages
   1. Developmental life stages
   2. Situational flashbacks

Results

As of 1987, 12 training sessions on parenting the sexually abused child had been conducted, and 65 families had been trained. This total includes 11 foster families who either requested the training or were asked to attend by their foster care worker. Of the 54 adoptive families who attended, 37 have had children placed in their homes. Twelve families did not complete the adoption study, withdrawing for various reasons (changes in family circumstances, deciding against adoption of special-needs children, etc.). Only one family withdrew because of the training on parenting the sexually abused child, and this couple (who had been married 14 years) reported that they had learned more about each other's feelings and attitudes toward sex and sexuality in one day of training than they had discovered in all their years of marriage. They asked that their study be put on hold until they had a chance to get to know each other all over again, and recently asked that they again be considered for the adoption program. Five of the families who have received the training are in the final phases of the study process, with placement of children in their homes expected within the next several months.

The 54 adoptive families who attended the training were assessed by inquiry forms and the pretest and post-test interviews regarding (1) their acceptance of the child's history of sexual abuse; and (2) their personal feelings of competence in parenting a sexually abused child. The families were separated into three categories based on their responses. The first category comprised those who expressed acceptance of the child's history of sexual abuse and felt confident of their ability to parent a sexually abused child. The second category was comprised of those who were accepting of the child's history, but expressed concern regarding their ability to parent a sexually abused child. The third category was made up of those who expressed difficulty in accepting the child's history of sexual abuse and doubted their ability to parent a sexually abused child adequately.

The authors identified statements such as: "I can't believe that people really do that to children"; "I always hear that children make up a lot of stories about sexual abuse"; or "Isn't that really just fantasy based on the child really wanting to take the parent's place with the other parent?" as indicators of the applicants' inability to accept the child's actual sexual abuse history. Statements such as: "I don't know how those children could ever be normal"; "They (the children) will always be different"; or "I don't know what we would do with a sexually abused child"; were indicators of doubt regarding the applicant's ability to parent sexually abused children.

The pretest revealed that 25 families (46%) were in category one, 20 families (38%) were in category two, and nine families (16%) were in category three, in terms of acceptance of the child's history of sexual abuse and feeling of competence in parenting a sexually abused child. After completing the training session, 50 of the adoptive families (93%) expressed both an acceptance of the child's history of sexual abuse and a feeling of competence in parenting a sexually abused child (category one). Four families (7%) indicated that they were accepting of the child's history of sexual abuse but continued to express doubt regarding their ability (or desire) to parent a sexually abused child (category two). No families were in the third category after the training.

Since 1983, we have placed 57 children with families who have received training in parenting sexually abused children. One child was placed with a family which had not been trained, for a total of 58 children placed into adoption. Three of the first adoptive placements disrupted, but the children were immediately re-placed with another trained adoptive family.

Of the 58 children placed into adoption, nine were infants either at the time they were placed into adoption or at the time they were placed with the foster parents who eventually adopted them. The remaining 49 children we have classified as special-needs children placed into adoption, and 42 (86%) have a history of some type of sexual abuse.

This figure of 86% is higher than the figures generally reported in the literature on sexual abuse. However, this is the same percentage (86%) as that for the children placed in a local emergency shelter during the four-year period from 1978 through 1981 who had an identified history of sexual abuse. That these figures correspond so exactly is highly significant, we feel, for all child placement specialists, whether they work in the field of foster care, residential treatment, or special-needs adoption.

Of the 42 sexually abused children placed into adoption since 1983, only 18 (43%) had a documented history of sexual abuse. Stated another way, fully 57% of the children placed with adoptive families had never revealed the sexual abuse to foster parents, case workers, or therapists; or, if they did tell someone, it was not documented in the child's records.

Of those 18 children who did have a known history of sexual abuse, one-third received no specialized treatment for sexual abuse victims. The overriding reason for this lack of treatment was that these children were not identified as primary victims; rather, they were siblings of the primary victim and the sexual abuse within the family system was not believed by caseworkers to have affected these children—in spite of the fact that every one of these siblings was involved in sexual behavior with the primary victims. This included a three-month-old infant who was repeatedly fondled by her five-year-old brother until they were separated in foster care over a year later. The foster parents could not understand why this 18-month-old child exhibited abnormal masturbatory behavior until we began working with the child a year later in preparation for adoptive placement. Although the research and published studies emphasize that sexual abuse occurs in the most dysfunctional families and that all family members are affected by the sexual abuse whether or not they are directly victimized, we continue to find siblings overlooked in treatment. This is more remarkable, we feel, since of the 10 sexually abused sibling groups we have placed with adoptive families, eight are now known to have engaged in some type of sibling sexual behavior ranging from mutual fondling to intercourse. These eight sibling groups represented 23 of the 27 children in the 10 sexually abused sibling groups placed.

In all eight cases of sibling sexual activity, the sexual behavior among the siblings began while the children were with the sexually abusing biological family and continued during foster care placement. Additionally, these children frequently involved other children in the foster home in their sexual games, teaching their sex games to the foster parents' grandchildren, nieces, and nephews who visited briefly. In spite of this almost constant sexual behavior (as reported by the children themselves), only one of the 23 children in these eight sibling groups received any treatment regarding the sexual acting out before their involvement in the adoption process.

Of the 49 special-needs children placed in adoption, 12 experienced disruption of the adoptive placement, with one 15-year-old boy having two disrupted placements, for a total of 13 disruptions (26%). Of those children who experienced an adoption disruption, three children were placed with a second adoptive family without reentering the foster care system, and this placement has been successful. Of the 10 children who reentered the foster care system, five were successfully placed with either a second adoptive family or with a relative. The adolescent boy who experienced the two disruptions has been able to establish a trust relationship with the second adoptive family and sees this family as his "ally" and "safe place." The first adoptive family, which is financially secure, has offered to finance any college or career-oriented training he might choose. There are, therefore, five children of the original 12 who experienced disruption who are not currently in a permanent situation.

Of the 12 children who experienced disruption, only two did not have a history of sexual abuse. These two were siblings who were placed with a couple who separated and divorced after the children were placed; and although both parents wanted to keep the children as a single parent, neither was emotionally nor financially stable during the period of the separation and divorce and they felt that removal would be in the best interests of the children. (Interestingly, both parents have maintained contact with the adoption program, and the wife has now reapplied to adopt as a single parent.)

For the ten who experienced disruption, the assessment of the reasons for the disruptions by both the families and the authors revealed that for eight of the 10 children, the previous sexual abuse and its impact did contribute to the disruption. In the one placement of two sexually abused sisters where the sexual abuse was not a factor, the adoptive mother had not wanted more children but had convinced herself that to be a good wife she needed to accede to her husband's desire for a larger family. The remaining eight sexually abused children whose placements disrupted were over ten years old and included three girls and five boys; all eight children had long-term histories of sexual abuse, and at least six had been molested more times than they could remember by more people than they could name. Although all these children were highly sexualized and most of them engaged in sexual activity after adoptive placement, including sibling incest, the adoptive parents were for the most part able to deal with these behaviors effectively. Rather, it was the secondary collaterals of sexual abuse—the child's inability to trust parents; anger and resentment expressed toward the parents, especially the mothers; and pressures from the community regarding the child's behavior—combined with the significant changes in the adoptive families' circumstances, that led to the disruption. (One family opened a new business about the time of the adoption placement, another lost their dairy farm, and in another adoptive family the father lost his job.) Most of the parents expressed the feeling that they had "just been worn down finally" by the overall pressures on the family combined with the child's behaviors and their own feelings of futility at being "unable to get through" to the child.

Our experience with disruption does correspond to the literature, which reports that the earlier the sexual abuse begins, the longer it continues; the more assaultive the sexual abuse, and the larger the number of perpetrators, the more difficult it is for the child and the family to overcome. The question remains, however, if these families had remained stable in other areas, would they have been able to deal effectively with the issues associated with the sexual abuse and would they have avoided disruption?

Other adoptive families of sexually abused children experienced similar major changes in the family circumstances and still managed to maintain the adoptive placement. Indeed, some of those same children who were the most victimized and whose first placements disrupted have been successfully incorporated into second adoptive families who also experienced major changes or circumstances.

Case Studies

To more fully illustrate the types of families who are able to parent sexually abused children successfully and the types of problems these children bring to the placement, the following three families are presented: *(1)* a family who adopted a sibling group of three sexually abused boys ages 10 to 14; *(2)* a family who adopted a sibling group of three sexually abused children ages three to six; and *(3)* a family who adopted a six-year-old sexually abused girl. All names have been changed.

The Elder Family

The Elder family consisted of the parents, both 35 years old, and their three daughters—Mary, 12; Jan, nine; and Sally, six. They lived on the outskirts of a very small community; the father worked as an engineer and the mother was a full-time housewife. They were unable to have more children, but they had always wanted a larger family. They saw a "Wednesday's Child" program that featured Ray, 14; Jack, 13; and Chris, 10. The Elders inquired about adopting the three boys and completed the group training for adoptive parents. Although there was no mention of the possibility of sexual abuse in the boys' histories, the Elders were asked to attend the next workshop regarding sexual abuse. This workshop, which was provided through agency contract, focused on the dynamics of sexual abuse and its effects on the child. The Elders attended this workshop the first weekend after the boys were placed in their home.

The boys had been in foster care for approximately two years before the adoptive placement. They had been removed from their biological parents with their younger sister, age nine, because of long-term gross neglect and lack of supervision. The boys were never placed with their sister because her behavior was highly disruptive, and she was placed in a residential treatment facility about the time the boys were placed into adoption since her behavior had become uncontrollable in the foster home.

Shortly after removal from the biological parents, Ray was placed in a residential treatment facility because of severe depression combined with a high level of nonspecific anger. After about a year in residential treatment, Ray was placed in the foster home with Jack and Chris. The three boys spent approximately a year together in the foster home before they were placed with the Elders.

Although none of the boys had ever disclosed any previous sexual abuse, their family history and the reactions of both Ray and their sister in foster care indicated that there was a high probability that there had been some type of sexual abuse. Additionally, shortly after placement with the elders, Ray again began displaying a great deal of anger, focused primarily on Mrs. Elder, combined with periods of depression and withdrawal. The Elders agreed with the adoption specialist that Ray had been sexually abused; however, Ray would not talk about it, even with the adoptive father, with whom he had developed the closest relationship. Ray was referred to a child psychiatrist, who interviewed him along with Jack and Chris, and then spoke with the Elders. The psychiatrist also agreed that Ray, and probably Jack and Chris, had been sexually abused, but he recommended that the issue not be confronted: "Ray will let you know when he's ready to talk about it."

The Elders legally consummated the boys' adoption about seven months after placement, and a couple of months after the adoption was legalized they discovered that the three boys had all been involved sexually with the three girls. The sexual involvement varied, with Ray and Mary establishing more of a boyfriend-girlfriend relationship in which the other boys were not involved. The relationship with Jan, who was the same age as the boys' biological sister, involved extremely complex dynamics, but the sexual behavior contained the classic elements of sexual abuse: primary perpetrator (Ray); a primary victim (Jan); collusion by other family members with each having a role to play (all the children in the family); an enticement and psychological/emotional pressure used to maintain continuing abuse; accessibility of the victim; and a determined plan to maintain the secret and keep the parents from finding out. Sally was the least involved of all the children; when she was approached to join the games, she thought it sounded "ucky" and ran away.

The Elders contacted the agency for assistance in working through the problems, asserting that any solution that involved removing any or all of the boys was unacceptable. Their attitude was that they were a family and they would work through the problems as a family. Indeed, the fear that the boys would be moved contributed to the girls not telling the parents about the sexual activity. The services provided to the family included individual and joint interviews with all family members and family sessions designed by the authors to assist the family in understanding and accepting what had happened, to help them learn to restructure the inappropriate sexual behavior, and to institute personal and family safeguards to prevent the inappropriate sexual behavior from resurfacing. The individual and joint interviews with the boys focused on their earlier sexual abuse (which had been extensive and had included sexual activity with their younger sister), to help them understand how their earlier victimization had resulted in their repeating the sexual abuse in their new family. Within eight weeks, the Elders felt confident that the sexual activity between the children was no longer occurring and that the family had the structures in place that would allow them to identify and work through any additional problems that might arise.

The Elders case dramatically demonstrates that sexual abuse does have a profound impact on children. Ray, Jack, and Chris had been sexually abused many, many times by different persons. Ray had suffered the most since he had been a "bastard" child; he was never accepted by his stepfather and, indeed, his mother "gave" him to a truck driver when he was five years old who "returned" him about a year later. Continuing sexual abuse, combined with rejection and family scapegoating, left him angry and depressed. Even after a year of treatment in a residential setting, a second year of placement in an excellent foster home, and almost a year with an adoptive family absolutely determined to love him, he was physically and emotionally incapable of repeating "I am a good person." His unshakable view of himself and his world was all bad and he tried to prove how worthless he was by involving the other children in the family sexual activity. Also, by taking the role of the perpetrator, Ray was finally in control; he associated the role of perpetrator with power, and this role allowed him to be in charge.

Another important factor was sexualization. Ray, Jack, and Chris had been involved in daily sexual activity for most of their lives, and this included sibling sexual activity. In fact, Jack (the talker of the group) reported that sometimes they would have sex with their sister because "for awhile it made us forget how hungry we were." The day Jack learned that not everyone had sex with their sister (he was seven years old) remains absolutely vivid in his memory.

The Elders' case also demonstrates the betrayal that sexually abused children feel. Ray, Jack, and Chris learned early that parents cannot be trusted to love, protect, and provide for children. The boys made the adoptive parents prove again and again that they would continue to love them no matter what, and the boys said that they "knew" that they would be "sent away when Mom and Dad found out" about the sexual activity with the girls. Jack said, "We knew they'd have to get rid of us then." When their parents refused to allow the boys to leave their family, the boys finally began to learn what a family is and what it meant to be a part of a family. It was then that the healing could begin.

The Elders were able to work through the problems encountered as a result of the placement of sexually abused children because they possessed both the personal attributes and the parenting skills the situation demanded. Both were absolutely committed to parenting, and they believed they were good parents. Both were also open-minded where their children were concerned. In those instances in which their religious and personal values conflicted with what was best for the children, they chose the needs of their children every time and reexamined their values.

The Elders also were able to understand the dynamics of sexual abuse; within a year after the boys were placed, they were able to accept that all of their children had a history of some type of sexual abuse. The Elders firmly believed, however, that this did not have to be forever damaging. Their attitude, which was frequently communicated, was "This has happened; we will deal with it and go on with our lives."

The skills the parents employed were *(1)* open communication on all levels with all the children; *(2)* the ability to provide structure and supervision; *(3)* the ability to role model appropriate behavior; and *(4)* the ability to use crisis as an opportunity for personal and family growth.

The boys were placed with the Elders in April 1983, and the family remains intact. In fact, the Elders later adopted another sexually abused boy of 16 whose first adoptive placement disrupted. Ray, Jack, and Chris are fully integrated members of the family and all three boys now excel in school. Ray is a recognized tennis star and one of the most popular boys in the school; Jack wants to be an engineer "just like Dad" and appears to have the natural abilities to succeed in this; Chris plans to be a millionaire before he is 30 and everyone who knows him believes absolutely that he will achieve his goal. Mary is an attractive teenager gifted in sports, music, and math, who wants to be either a teacher or a psychologist; Jan has become an assertive but feminine 13-year-old who is choosing between first boyfriends; and Sally has finally decided she is ready to grow up and not be the baby of the family any more.

As a result of the family's experiences, the Elders have become leading advocates of the adoption of special-needs children, and it sometimes seem they have established their own center for sexual abuse victims, since the children frequently bring home other children "who need to talk to Mom and Dad." All of the children view themselves as advocates and protectors of other children, and their experiences have led them to be particularly sensitive to potentially dangerous situations and people. The Elders believe that children can be healed in adoption—not without pain and heartache—and they never hesitate to share this message and their story.

The Strong Family

The Strong family was originally just the wife, 31 and the husband, 30. They were unable to have children but had always seen themselves as parents to two or three children. The Strongs completed the adoption group training and the six-hour training for parenting sexually abused children.

The Strongs were selected for the placement of Joyce (age five), Matt (age four), and John (age three), who were available for adoption in another part of the state. The three children had been removed from the biological family two years earlier because of gross neglect, with John having earlier been hospitalized for failure to thrive. Joyce and John were placed in the same foster home and Matt lived in another foster home nearby. After about a year, Joyce began fondling John and another foster child in the home. She then revealed that she had been sexually abused by her father before placement, and that he continued to fondle and penetrate her with his fingers during the weekly court-ordered visits. Joyce began regular play therapy sessions, but her sexual acting-out behavior increased. She was described as "preoccupied with sex" and fondled not only the other foster children in the home but also tried to fondle the children in her preschool. The foster parent was unable to control this behavior, and Joyce, at age four, was placed in a residential treatment facility for emotionally disturbed children.

Matt and John were ready for adoptive placement, however, so the Strongs were asked if they would accept the two boys first, visit regularly with Joyce, and then accept her when she was ready to be discharged from treatment. The Strongs readily agreed and followed through with the plans, traveling approximately 150 miles to the treatment facility several times to visit Joyce. They also brought her home for weekend and holiday visits.

Matt and John adjusted easily to the Strongs' home, and John displayed no negative signs from the earlier fondling by Joyce. Soon after placement the adoptive parents began using games to teach the boys self-protection techniques. The parents recognized that being with John and Matt could trigger Joyce's old habits, although there had been no reports of sexual acting out at the treatment facility; before Joyce's first overnight visit they reviewed the self-protection techniques, talked with the boys about Joyce's having learned some inappropriate games, and practiced how the situation should be handled if Joyce wanted them to play these games. During the frequent and extended visits there were no instances of inappropriate sexual behavior.

After about nine months, the treatment facility staff members felt that Joyce was ready for adoptive placement. They were especially pleased with the progress that Joyce had made as a result of the contact with the Strongs, remarking that she had become more assertive and had developed excellent self-protective techniques. On one occasion Joyce reported to staff members that a little boy was behaving inappropriately with other little girls. Asked where she had learned to identify inappropriate behavior and how to deal with it, Joyce said that the Strongs had taught her that "those kinds of games were not good games for little children to play and I should say No! if someone wants to play like that." The placing agency felt, however, that Joyce would "always be a potential threat" to her brothers and decided not to place Joyce with her brothers in the Strongs' home. The Strongs nevertheless refused to accept this forecasting of Joyce's future, and they eventually succeeded in having Joyce placed with their family.

The primary problems encountered after placement of Joyce with the family involved rebuilding appropriate sibling relationships, establishing parent-child roles, and assisting Joyce in working through the anger associated with the original sexual abuse. As is typical, the primary focus of the anger was the mother.

The Strongs were able to work through these problems by providing structured activities for the children with clearly stated expectations. They repeated the expectations and the role definitions constantly, helping Joyce to understand the difference between parental roles and responsibilities, and the role of the big sister. Mrs. Strong helped Joyce work through the anger by recognizing and accepting it and by patiently helping Joyce to slowly learn to differentiate between anger toward the "old" mother and anger toward her. Both parents happily supplied the holding and cuddling Joyce desperately needed, teaching her to substitute this appropriate touching for the inappropriate sexual touch. Finally, Mrs. Strong openly and honestly supplied Joyce with the factual information about sex and sexuality necessary for her to understand what had happened to her. Mrs. Strong reported that she "was amazed" at how limited Joyce's knowledge of sex and sexuality was "in spite of the fact that she had experienced so much." By dealing with the subject openly and honestly, she was able to help Joyce begin to view sex as "something neat between grown-ups who love each other—like Mommy and Daddy!" instead of an experience filled with pain and fear.

The three children are now all legally members of the Strong family. There have been no instances of inappropriate sexual behavior, and the three children "fuss and fight like all brothers and sisters." The Strongs are aware that "Joyce will always be affected by what happened to her," but they believe that this has not permanently "damaged" her in any way; instead, they believe that "a part of our job as parents is to help her keep the sexual abuse in perspective as she grows and changes." The Strongs believe that "giving all the love you can give is really important," but the mother adds, "You also have to keep the lines of communication open. As long as we can talk, we can deal with any problem that comes up, and it's our job to make sure that those communication lines are always open so Joyce feels comfortable telling or asking us anything."

THE LEED FAMILY

The Leed family was composed of the father, age 40; the mother, age 38; and their biological daughter Cathy, 12. Both parents had families of origin with eight or more siblings. Their extended families were close, family-oriented, and active in community and church activities. Cathy was outgoing, a leader at school, church, and among her cousins, and she had a deep desire for "my own little sister." The Leeds were unable to have more children of their own. They had seen a special-needs child on the local "Wednesday's Child" program and they responded, requesting they be considered for that child. Although they were not selected for that child, they were willing to consider another special-needs child.

Nancy, age six, came from a background of severe physical abuse, and she had permanent scarring from extension cords and switches. She had been in foster care since she was three years old. Nancy had been placed once before in adoption with a single parent, and after one year of preconsummation placement she was returned to the agency when the adoptive mother called and simply said, "Come get Nancy." She would give no reason for the removal, why there had been no previous indications of problems, or why she wanted the child removed immediately. The agency felt that the mother's new boyfriend may have been the reason for Nancy's return to the agency.

Following the adoption disruption, Nancy had three foster home placements. She was described by these foster parents as rejecting, hateful, and hard to discipline. Nancy was also believed to be mentally retarded because she rarely spoke, had little affect, and kept herself apart from others. She also demonstrated hostile, threatening behavior whenever approached, mumbling, "I'll kill you," or "Leave me alone" in a "spooky" tone of voice.

Nancy was moved to a skilled and tenured foster family who agreed to help the agency assess the child's functioning and her ability to relate to an adoptive family. It was suspected by the adoption specialist that Nancy had been sexually abused and so from the beginning, the foster parents forced Nancy to talk and look at them directly, reinforced that she was lovable and good, and gave her verbal and nonverbal messages that she was safe and would be protected. By the end of the first two weeks, Nancy was verbally expressing anger at the foster parents and her fear of men, and she cried easily when frustrated. One night (as usual) Nancy refused to go to bed, and she began throwing tantrums and crawling under the bed. The foster mother picked her up and began to rock her, talking with her about her fear of being molested and not being able to protect herself. Nancy began to cry, and she cried nonstop all night. The next day, although exhausted, she clung to the foster family members, who continued to hold and rock her all day. Whenever she fell asleep, she would have nightmares that woke her up, and she would begin to cry again. During the second night, Nancy was held and rocked again until her sobbing was finally reduced to fretfulness. The foster family continued to respond to the child's traumatic reaction with words of comfort, reassurance, and the promise of safety.

The following day Nancy began to interact with the foster family openly. Although weak, she was talking, asking questions, and occasionally she laughed. At first she felt safe only in the kitchen and the family room with the rocking chair. She finally expanded the safety area to the rest of the house, and at the end of the fourth week she was confident enough to play outside in the back yard as long as someone was within hearing distance.

After the three-day traumatic reaction, Nancy began to show other indicators of sexual abuse. She tried to fondle the foster father several times when she was under stress, and to act out various sex acts with her three-year-old foster sister. Sometimes when alone with the foster mother, she would give indirect clues to the past abuse, saying in a low voice "suck my dick" and "I'm going to fuck you." Responding to the boundaries and limits set by the foster parents, however, she began to demonstrate more appropriate behavior. The foster parents emphasized appropriate parent-child behavior, ways of expressing affection within a family, and helped Nancy feel safe from further sexual abuse by constantly reassuring her and helping her to learn to protect herself.

The Leeds had been interested in and accepting of Nancy when she had been considered mentally retarded; and as work with Nancy progressed, the adoption specialist began involving the Leeds through weekly updates and later by encouraging the Leeds to talk to the foster parents directly. It became apparent that Nancy was not mentally retarded, but emotionally upset due to past sexual abuse. The Leeds attended the sexual abuse training for adoptive parents and began reading related books and other literature. They were aware of and sensitive to Nancy's recent reaction to having been abused. They understood Nancy's need for support and behavioral education in the four areas most affected by sexual abuse, especially sexuality, powerlessness, and trust.

At the first meeting between Nancy and the Leeds, emphasis was placed on Nancy's traumatic past and her need for safety and security. The Leeds responded with reassurance and specifically explained how children in their family were protected. Mr. Leed explained how he related to children and identified parent-child role boundaries in his home and family system. Mrs. Leed identified her need and feeling of responsibility to provide her children with proper supervision and protection. The Leeds encouraged Nancy to allow herself to become a part of their family, and the foster family encouraged Nancy to trust the Leeds, identifying them as a family that supported and protected children. Issues related to the sexual abuse were discussed, such as Nancy's nightmares, fear of the bedroom, fear of discipline, and the need to hide when unknown men were present. The Leeds explored with Nancy and the foster parents different ways to handle these situations, with Nancy telling the plans of action she preferred and the new ideas she thought would work.

When Nancy visited in the Leed home, family rules for child protection were emphasized to encourage Nancy to feel safe ("Play in the backyard," "If you go out the front door, you have to tell someone," and "Never leave the front yard"). Cathy with her parents' support, talked to Nancy about how to protect herself if a parent was out of reach. Night safety was also discussed and role-playing was done to teach Nancy ways of dealing with her night fears. Nancy was reassured of the importance of children to the Leed family through observation, family members' responses, and the established boundaries and rules of a family that protected children.

The Leed placement reflects not only the traumatic impact of sexual abuse, but also how essential it is for the adoptive family to help the victim establish basic feelings of safety and security. Children must have these needs met before they can continue normal development, and parents are the primary resource for helping children feel safe and secure. The Leeds began this process with Nancy by emphasizing (*1*) clear and concise role boundaries of the parents and the children; and (*2*) the responsibility of the family to provide protection for its children and to teach them how to protect themselves. The Leeds understood Nancy's fears and worked to overcome them. Providing structure, security, and open communication at the beginning of the placement led to an easier adjustment for Nancy and to the alleviation of unnecessary fear and distancing. The Leeds understood Nancy's need to develop age-appropriate social and educational skills, recognizing that in the past, Nancy's emotional energy was focused on self-protection and survival. The Leeds accepted Nancy at her developmental stage, and they provided her with the encouragement, support, and resources to begin achievement in other areas.

After the initial testing stage when Nancy was trying to re-create the abusive situation, her development of social and educational skills was rapid. Cathy, as normally happens in the adoption process as the family adjusts to incorporate new members, experienced anger, depression, and rebellion for about six weeks. A contributing factor to her reaction was the amount of time and attention the parents had to devote to Nancy during the first few months after placement. However, after Cathy and the parents were helped to understand the reasons for Cathy's feeling left out, the family included Cathy in helping Nancy become a member of the family. Cathy is now doing well and is proud and protective of her little sister. The parents are delighted with Nancy and her accomplishments. Their question now is "How about a little boy?"

Recommendations for Further Research

Four areas in particular could benefit from further study. One is the identification of sexual abuse victims and the reasons sexual abuse is so often not recognized by helping professionals. This should include more detailed study of the sexual behaviors of victims, the frequency of the abuse, its effects on the child, and associated sibling sexual activities.

Treatment of sexual abuse victims is the second area for study, focusing on determining the most effective means of restructuring their behavior as to sexuality, trust, self-image, and control over their environment.

Third is the identification of the characteristics of adoptive families that enable them to successfully incorporate sexually abused children into the family system. The first phase would be determining which personal and family attributes make some families good candidates for accepting sexually abused children, and the second phase would be identification of those qualities that contribute to maintaining the placement when crises occur.

The final area needing further study is the effects on the child of removal from the abusive family system as compared to the effects on the child of remaining in the abusive family and receiving treatment. Many programs are now in place that provide services to the sexually abusive family, and many other programs provide services to children removed from the family system. Because of the varied treatment approaches and the lack of an organized research effort, little information is available regarding the long-term effectiveness of these programs. A longitudinal comparison study could clarify whether we are saving today's family while creating tomorrow's dysfunctional adults. In regard to the children removed from the abusive family and placed in adoption, the question becomes "What sexually abused children can adoption be expected to heal, and for what children would the cost of failure be too great?" A comparison of the two groups could throw more light than we now have on the effectiveness of the treatment programs and the relative necessity of adoption as the treatment of choice, given the possibility of the children's being freed for adoption.

References

Adams-Tucker, J.C. "Proximate Effects of Sexual Abuse in Childhood: A Report on 28 Children." *American Journal of Psychiatry* 139 (1982): 1252–1256.

Barth, R.P.; Berry, M.; Carson, M.L.; Goodfield, R.; and Feinburg, B. "Contributors to Disruption and Dissolution of Older-Child Adoptions." *Child Welfare* LXV (July/August 1986): 359–371.

Bass, Ellen. "Introduction: In the Truth Itself, There is Healing." In *I Never Told Anyone: Writings by Women Survivors of Child Sexual Abuse*, edited by Ellen Bass and Louise Thornton. New York: Harper & Row, 1983.

Borgman, Robert. "Problems of Sexually Abused Girls and Their Treatment." *Social Casework* (March 1984): 182–187.

Browne, Angela, and Finkelhor, David. "Impact of Child Sexual Abuse: A Review of The Research." *Psychological Bulletin* 90 (1986): 66–67.

Burgess, Ann, and Holmstrom, Lynda. "Accessory-to-Sex: Pressure, Sex, and Secrecy" In *Sexual Assault of Children and Adolescents*, edited by Ann W. Burgess *et al.* Lexington, MA: Lexington Books, D.C. Heath and Company, 1978.

Cohen, Tamar. "The Incestuous Family Revisited." *Social Casework* (March 1983): 154–161.

Conte, R., Jr., and Berliner, Lucy. "Sexual Abuse of Children: Implications for Practice." *Social Casework* 62 (1981): 601–606

Damon, Linda; Todd, Judith; and McFarland, Kee. "Treatment Issues with Sexually Abused Young Children." *Child Welfare* LXVI (March/April 1987) 125–137.

Duehn, Wayne. "Helping the Sexually Abused Child in Adoption/Foster Care." Workshop presented to adoptive and foster parents. Longview, TX, July 9, 1984.

Elwell, Mary E. "Sexually Assualted Children and Their Families." *Social Casework* (April 1979): 227–235.

Festinger, Trudy. *Necessary Risk: A Study of Adoptions and Disrupted Adoptive Placements.* Washington, DC: Child Welfare League of America, Inc., 1986.

Finkelhor, David, and Browne, Anglea. "The Traumatic Impact of Child Sexual Abuse." *American Journal of Orthopsychiatry* 55 (October 1985): 530–543.

Fowler, Carol; Burns, Susan; and Roehl, Janet. "Against Sexual Assault, Phoenix, Arizona Counseling the Incest Offender." *International Journal of Family Therapy* 5 (Summer 1983): 92–97.

Groth, A. Nicholas. "Patterns of Sexual Assault Against Children and Adolescents." In *Sexual Assault of Children and Adolescents*," edited by Ann W. Burgess *et al.* Lexington, MA: Lexington Books, D.C. Heath and Co., 1978a.

Groth, A. Nicholas. "Guidelines for the Assessment and Management of the Offender." In *Sexual Assault of Children and Adolescents,* edited by Ann W. Burgess *et. al.* Lexington, MA: Lexington Books, D.C. Heath and Co., 1978b.

Groth, A. Nicholas; Hobson, Williams; and Gary, Thomas. "The Incest Offender." In *Handbook of Clinical Intervention in Child Sexual Abuse,* edited by Suzanne M. Sgroi. Lexington, MA: Lexington Books, D.C. Heath and Co., 1982.

Hoorwitz, Aaron N. "Guidelines for Treating Father-Daughter Incest." *Social Casework* (November 1983): 515–524

Jewett, Claudia L. *Adopting the Older Child.* Cambridge, MA: The Harvard Common Press, 1978.

Katz, Linda. "Parental Stress and Factors for Success in Older Child Adoptions." *Child Welfare* LXV (November/December 1986): 569–578

Krenk, Christopher. "Training Residence Staff for Child Abuse Treatment." *Child Welfare* LXIII (March/April 1984): 167–173

Lanyon, Richard L. Theory and Treatment in Child Molestation." *Journal of Consulting and Clinical Psychology* 54 (1986): 176–182

Lee, Judith A.B. and Rosenthal, Susan J. "Working with Victims of Violent Assault." *Social Casework* (December1983): 593–601

———. "Reports Differ on Cuts." *Longview Morning Journal* (March 1, 1987): 1A, 8A

McCarty, Loretta M. "Mother-Child Incest: Characteristics of the Offender." *Child Welfare* LXV (September/October 1986): 447–458

Nelson, Katherine A. *On the Frontier of Adoption: A Study of Special Needs Adoptive Families.* Washington, DC: Child Welfare League of America, Inc., 1985.

Sarafino, Edward P. "An Estimate of Nationwide Incidences of Sexual Offenses Against Children." *Child Welfare* LXIII: (February 1979): 127–134

Sgroi, Suzanne M. "Child Sexual Assault" Some Guidelines for Intervention and Assessment. In *Sexual Assault of Children and Adolescents,* edited by Ann W. Burgess *et al.* Lexington, MA: Lexington Books, D.C. Heath and Company, 1978a.

———. "A National Needs Assessment for Protecting Child Victims of Sexual Assault." In *Sexual Assault of Children and Adolescents,* edited by Ann W. Burgess *et al.* Lexington, MA: Lexington Books, D.C. Heath and Company, 1978b.

———. "Introduction: The State of the Art in Child Sexual Abuse Interreaction." In *Handbook of Clinical Intervention in Child Sexual Abuse,* edited by Suzanne M. Sgroi. Lexington, MA: Lexington Books, D.C. Heath and Company, 1982.

———. "Sexual Molestation of Children." *Children Today* 4 (1975): 19-21.

Shultz, Leroy G. "Sexual Victims." In *The Sexually Oppressed,* edited by Harvey L. Gochros and Jan S. Gochros. New York: Associated Press, 1977.

———. Texas Department of Human Resource, Child Protective Service Handbook, 1985.

Timmons-Mitchell, Jane "Containing Agressive Acting Out in Abused Children." *Child Welfare* LXV (September/October 1986): 459–468.

Viorst, Judith. *Necessary Losses.* New York: Simon and Schuster, 1986.

Weinbach, Robert W., and Curtiss, Christina R. "Making Child Abuse Victims Aware of Their Victimization: A Treatment Issue." *Child Welfare* LXV (July/August 1986): 337–346

The Authors

Deborah H. Minshew has worked with Child Protective Services, Texas Department of Human Services, since 1974. She has specialized in children in the substitute care system (foster care and adoption) with histories of sexual abuse. She is currently a Regional Adoption Specialist placing special-needs children.

Ms. Minshew received her M.S.S.W. from the University of Texas at Arlington.

Chrisan Hooper worked with Child Protective Services, Texas Department of Human Services, for 10 years. She was a Regional Adoption Specialist for five years. She currently resides in Germany and is employed by the Department of Defense Family Advocacy Program.

Ms. Hooper received her B.S. from Austin College and her M.S.S.W. from the University of Texas at Arlington.